I loved this book [...]
his own illness, h [...]
writes clearly and [...]
about the reality [...] *ly honest*
important insights about how to survive it. Though it is filled
with sa [...]

Eati [...]
indivi [...]
abo [...]
pers [...]

Ja [...]

Mar [...]
manne [...]
on the [...]
A movin [...]
less [...]
or ho [...]
other [...]

Pri [...]

The [...]
his stor [...]
l [...]
wh [...]

G [...]

Mark's touching but no holds barred account of mental health issues is delivered with great honesty and humour.
It offers many real insights on how to interact with those facing mental health challenges, whether emotional, physical, financial or even legal.
Antony Morris: Head of Dispute Resolution at Clarks legal law firm

The loneliness suffered by mental health sufferers is the biggest epidemic of our time. Great to see this book tackling the issue of mental health head-on, a key priority for us in the company and for myself personally. Highly engaging book and very relatable.
Leena Nair: Chief HR Officer at Unilever

Mark writes very honestly about his daughter's experience of anorexia. He doesn't claim to have all the answers but offers his own perspective on the war against the illness. He draws us in as if we are right there in his brain, painting such a vivid picture. Reading his messages to Emily while she was in hospitalbrought tears to my eyes. I couldn't put the book down.
Hope Virgo: Author of 'Stand Tall Little Girl'

Creating safe spaces around mental health issues in the workplace is at the heart of what we do. By baring his soul in an open, honest and often humorous way, Mark's book demonstrates bravery, courage and humility in bucketloads. If we all were to follow his lead, just imagine the change we could make together.
Gemma Greaves: Chief Executive at The Marketing Society

Mental health is the single most important challenge thattoday's leaders should be addressing in organisations.Mark's account gives us an important and courageous personal insight into the devastating impact of work-related stresswhich I hope leaders will take notice of.
Abi Marchant: Executive Coach and Former HR Director

www.triggerpublishing.com

Overcoming adversity and thriving

Breakdown and Repair
A Father's Tale of Stress and Success

BY MARK SIMMONDS

We are proud to introduce The**inspirational**series™. Part of the Trigger family of innovative mental health books, The**inspirational**series™ tells the stories of the people who have battled and beaten mental health issues. For more information visit: www.triggerpublishing.com

THE AUTHOR

During a career spanning 25 years, Mark has worked as a management trainer. He has run learning programmes in innovation and creativity for corporate giants like Unilever, GlaxoSmithkline, Philips and HSBC right across the globe. Along with his business partner Hanne Kristiansen, he now runs a small agency called Creative Creatures.

Throughout his life, Mark has struggled with pressure and anxiety, and suffered a nervous breakdown in 2001, brought on by work-related stress. During the last six years, Mark has utilised his experiences of mental ill health in his capacity as a carer, helping his daughter battle against anorexia nervosa.

His book, *Breakdown and Repair*, brings both episodes to life very openly and honestly. By collaborating with the young and talented illustrator, Lucy Streule, his aim is to make the topic of mental health accessible to all by exploring the light side of darkness.

First published in Great Britain 2019 by Trigger

Trigger is a trading style of Shaw Callaghan Ltd & Shaw Callaghan 23 USA, INC.

The Foundation Centre

Navigation House, 48 Millgate, Newark

Nottinghamshire NG24 4TS UK

www.triggerpublishing.com

Copyright © Mark Simmonds 2019

British Library Cataloguing in Publication Data

A CIP catalogue record for this book is available upon request
from the British Library

ISBN: 978-1-912478-99-6

This book is also available in the following e-Book and Audio formats:

MOBI: 978-1-78956-003-9

EPUB: 978-1-78956-001-5

PDF: 978-1-912478-72-9

AUDIO: 978-1-78956-004-6

Mark Simmonds has asserted his right under the Copyright,
Design and Patents Act 1988 to be identified as the author of this work

Cover design and typeset by Fusion Graphic Design Ltd

Printed and bound in Great Britain by Clays Ltd, Elcograf S.p.A

Paper from responsible sources

TRIGGER™

The mental health & wellbeing publisher

www.triggerpublishing.com

Thank you for purchasing this book.
You are making an incredible difference.

Proceeds from all Trigger books go directly to
The Shaw Mind Foundation, a global charity that focuses
entirely on mental health. To find out more about
The Shaw Mind Foundation visit,
www.shawmindfoundation.org

MISSION STATEMENT

Our goal is to make help and support available for every
single person in society, from all walks of life.
We will never stop offering hope. These are our promises.

Trigger and The Shaw Mind Foundation

the *Shaw* **mind**
FOUNDATION

Creating hope for children,
adults and families

A NOTE FROM THE SERIES EDITOR

The Inspirational range from Trigger brings you genuine stories about our authors' experiences with mental health problems.

Some of the stories in our Inspirational range will move you to tears. Some will make you laugh. Some will make you feel angry, or surprised, or uplifted. Hopefully they will all change the way you see mental health problems.

These are stories we can all relate to and engage with. Stories of people experiencing mental health difficulties and finding their own ways to overcome them with dignity, humour, perseverance and spirit.

Mark's story is not only one of strength and resilience but one that we can all relate to. Striving to climb higher and higher in the corporate world, while also supporting a family, can leave us all feeling burned out. In our modern times, becoming your own boss can seem enticing, but we rarely hear about the pressures that come with it. Mark writes candidly about this all, and also offers a touching narrative of how his daughter's battle with anorexia saved them both.

This is our Inspirational range. These are our stories. We hope you enjoy them. And most of all, we hope that they will educate and inspire you. That's what this range is all about.

Lauren Callaghan,
Co-founder and Lead Consultant Psychologist at Trigger

To Meli, Will, Em and Jack.

Disclaimer: Some names and identifying details have been changed to protect the privacy of individuals.

Trigger Warning: This book contains reference to suicide.

INTRODUCTION

18th July 2001

10pm on Wednesday evening and almost time for bed. I'm confronted by the army of usual suspects: the anti-depressants, the anti-anxiety pills, the sleeping tablets, and the new kids on the block – the anti-psychotics. The bathroom cabinet resembles a pharmacy and there seems to be a pill for almost every part of my life.

But please let me reassure you. I'm completely normal. I really am.

Extreme stress at work had brought on the panic attacks, which were soon followed by a mental breakdown and the onset of severe agitated depression. During this time, there was one aborted return to work, followed by just under four months' sick leave.

I've now seen six mental health specialists, including a counsellor, a hypnotherapist, an expensive Harley Street psychiatrist, and, at the suggestion of my mother-in-law, a retired faith healer. I've attended separate "coping with depression" and "coping with anxiety" courses, and have been a whisker away from being admitted into a local mental health unit in Aylesbury as an in-patient.

I'm becoming a danger both to myself and to my nearest and dearest.

But please, please believe me. I am completely normal.

I'm no longer communicating with either my wife or my three young children, even though we're all living under the same roof. I've lost any meaningful contact with everybody and anybody. I've dropped over 13 pounds in weight, my fingernails are bitten to the quick, and I am pretty convinced I've become impotent.

The following morning, I go cycling on my own down a country road. My brain feels like a jumble of spaghetti when I collide head-on with a 10-ton truck.

It appears I have tried to commit suicide.

Unsuccessfully.

I suffer serious head injuries as well as a collapsed lung and am transported by an air ambulance to the John Radcliffe Hospital in Oxford, where I spend two weeks recovering.

It is fair to say that, so far, it has not exactly been a vintage summer.

PART I

CHAPTER 1

SEEDS OF DESTRUCTION

It's in the Family

I blame my mother, Alice.

Alicja Pomiechowska was born in Kolno, Poland in 1933. During the Second World War, when she was eight years old, she fled across the border and ended up in Siberia along with her mother and younger brother. Her father was missing in action. They spent the rest of the war in misery, living in dire refugee camps where nobody really wanted them, existing more than living. But they survived.

When the war was over, her mother, Jadwiga, decided they would resettle in Kenya, one of the countries that had agreed to accept refugees.

So they moved, having lost everything in Poland.

Alice's teenage years were spent in poverty in the port of Mombasa. She took on the added responsibility of looking after her brother, Valdemar, while her mother worked as a nurse to earn the money they needed to live on. Alice learnt to speak English and eventually found work as a secretary in Nairobi, and it was there, years later, where she met and married my father, Peter. He was working for Pearl Assurance as a British expatriate. As far as Alice was concerned, it was a romantic ending of sorts to what had been an undeniably challenging start to life.

My brother and I were both born in Kenya, and the four of us moved back as a family to the UK in 1970. I was seven and my brother, Michael, was three. When we both left home for university in the 80s, my mother, then in her early fifties, suffered a severe nervous breakdown from which she never really recovered. The last 30 years of her life were spent in a "hermit-like" solitude, keeping well out of society's way as much as possible. She survived on a diet of anti-depressants, anti-anxiety pills, and sleeping tablets in an attempt to keep both the depression at bay and her nerves under control.

It's hard to believe her traumatic past was not a major contributing factor to the mental suffering she experienced when she entered middle age.

But here's the thing: her mother and brother had also endured the same hardships early on, no less painful, but they both remained mentally robust and well clear of any depressive illnesses. In fact, Jadwiga's adventures continued when she decided to emigrate to the USA. There, she met and married a Texan oilman called George, and lived happily and healthily until the ripe old age of 90. She was as tough as nails, not averse to taking risks. My grandmother was always inquisitive to know what lay around the next corner in life. My mother was not.

Did my mother simply draw the short straw? Did she inherit some "tricky" genes from somebody higher up in her family tree? And were these unluckily triggered by the challenging environments she found herself in at different stages of her life?

Just for the record, I'm only joking. I don't really blame my mother. I was very close to her because we were kindred spirits. We were cut from the same cloth. Over the years, I have noticed that there is often an affinity between people with shared experiences of either anxiety or depression. Without having to say very much, you instinctively know only too well what the other has been through or is going through. You completely get it, get them, and you become automatic members of the exclusive "Been to The Dark Side" club.

I have a similar relationship with my daughter, Emily, who became seriously ill with anorexia nervosa when she was 16. Although it was difficult to pin down the precise origins of her illness, it is generally recognised that high-achieving perfectionists are often susceptible to disorders like anxiety, depression, anorexia, and bulimia. Lauren Muhlheim, Psychologist and Certified Eating Disorder Specialist, highlights three specific domains of perfectionism that have been identified in literature: performance at work or school, close relationships, and physical appearance.[1] Emily sought perfection in all three.

Studies have shown that patients with anorexia nervosa and bulimia nervosa strive for higher levels of perfectionism than those without.[2]

All it took with Emily was the arrival of a perfect storm of external events, working in harmony to activate her perfectionist streak. Exam pressure, boyfriend issues, the death of a favourite school teacher, glandular fever, an eye-opening World Challenge trip to a poverty-stricken part of Ghana in Africa as well as some irrational body image problems were the catalysts. She was unable to take her A Level exams, spent a year in three eating disorder clinics, self-harmed, threatened suicide, and suffered from severe depression and anxiety. Her weight dropped to 70 pounds, and at her lowest point she had a tube inserted into her nose to give her the nutrition she needed to stay alive.

And yet her siblings, Will and Jack, were both exposed to the same environment and similar pressures. Neither of them (touch wood!) have shown any signs of a predisposition to mental health disorders.

I wonder, like Alice, did Emily get the duff draw from the gene pool? Was she dealt the joker in the pack?

My theory is my mother, my daughter, and I were all the unlucky ones from a genetic point of view, and that in each of our cases, our sleeping time-bombs were set off by a series of exceptional circumstances.

The three of us represent the fault line down through the family tree.

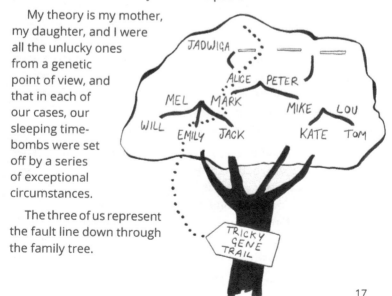

Before moving on, I must apologise to my wife, Melanie. She had to endure the damaging effects of the Simmonds' tricky gene in action across three successive generations. I don't think that's what she signed up for when she uttered the words 'I will' on a sunny Saturday afternoon back in May 1992. What made things even worse for her is that she had never experienced mental ill health before, either first- or second-hand. At least not as far as her immediate family was concerned. Panic attacks, breakdowns, depression, self-harming, and starving yourself to death were a complete mystery to her.

Mel was lucky, she was blessed with "happy genes".

And they would be sorely tested during the course of our marriage.

Introducing the Worry and Winner Genes

In the world's largest investigation into the impact of DNA on mental disorders, more than 200 researchers identified 44 gene variants that increase the likelihood of depression.[3] I am certainly not a scientist, nor a biologist, and I don't have the slightest interest in genetics. I was always more into the "fluffy" subjects at school like English and French, rather than the "hard as concrete" ones like mathematics and the sciences. But I think I might just have stumbled across 2 new gene variants to add to the 44. The first is called Worry and the second is called Winner. Having one or the other is generally okay, I think. But when both are deeply embedded in your DNA, it might just lead to some internal conflicts, and fireworks could go off.

There were undoubtedly some early warning signs during my teenage years that both Worry and Winner were in my blood. At school, I was a very conscientious student. I prepared myself well for exams, never leaving things until the last minute, always heavily dependent on strict and meticulous revision timetables. My peers would be burning the midnight oil, cramming in facts and figures, while I was tucked up in bed at 10pm, fully prepared for the challenges of the next day. This was a sign not of complacency, but one of extreme caution.

I acquired this characteristic from my father. Peter Simmonds was a very cautious man, and this manifested itself not only in the workplace but also at home. His weekends were metronomic in nature. Back home from London at half past six on a Friday. First whisky at seven. Last whisky at nine, followed by lightly poached eggs on toast. In bed by quarter past eleven. A walk on the Brighton seafront, first and last thing on Saturday, repeated on Sunday. Light stretching at the end of both days. Paperwork always filed away, every penny accounted for, slippers neatly in place, socks and underpants carefully ironed. Never late for anything. Ever. In fact, he was worse than that. He was a "you can never arrive too early" kind of person.

I was a lot like my father. I still am.

My mother was the worrier in the family and the permanent creases etched on her face were testament to this. She had three mechanisms for coping with daily stresses. She did her best to avoid any situations that brought uncertainty with them; she smoked like a chimney; and, later in her life, she resorted to a cocktail of anti-depressants and anti-anxiety pills to keep her nerves under control. Life seemed to be one perpetual challenge for Alice. A never-ending struggle. I suspect she could never quite escape the horrible memories of her childhood, spent in frightening and freezing Siberian refugee camps, where nothing ever remained certain for very long.

It was the combination of my father's caution and my mother's anxiety that ensured I was born with the "Worry" gene. But, of course, this was just one half of my tricky gene combination.

One of my other core personality traits was that I was always a very competitive person, academically, socially, and in the sporting arena. I was blessed with above average talent in several different team sports at school, including rugby and cricket, and competing and winning have always been important to me. I am not sure whether my aptitude for sport or my desire to win were a result of either nature or nurture. I suspect it was both.

So, not only was I burdened with the Worry gene, but I was also "blessed" with a very determined and ambitious "Winner" gene, the other tricky twin.

Unfortunately, these two, side-by-side as they were, did not always make for compatible partners. There were too many fundamental differences between them, in terms of what they valued and what they felt to be important. My high levels of anxiety and my inability to relax when under pressure meant I never quite fulfilled my potential, in particular on the sports field. I was occasionally let down by my mental fragility because I cared too much about losing and disappointing others. When my mind needed to be relaxed and focused in the heat of battle, it was often infiltrated with negative thoughts and irrational doubts, neither of which were conducive to the art of winning.

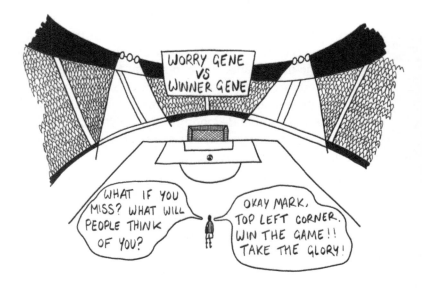

I would not have been the person to take the last-minute penalty to win the football World Cup final, serve out for the match in a tense fifth set in the men's final at Wimbledon or sink a difficult downhill 10-foot putt to win the US Masters Golf Tournament at Augusta. There would have been far too much distracting noise in my head.

All of this should have provided me with some early evidence that I would always need to manage my hopes and expectations carefully if the marriage between the two genes was going to remain a happy one.

When I grew up and entered the hurly burly world of business, I would find out just how important it was to balance the contrasting needs of both Worry and Winner genes.

One day in the distant future, not doing so would almost cost me my life.

CHAPTER 2

SQUARE PEG
IN A ROUND HOLE

MARK HAD ENTERED
THE LAND OF THE CORPORATE GIANTS

My First Little Blip in the Business World

In my early twenties, my Worry and Winner genes got their first proper examination when I started working for Unilever, the global consumer goods company co-headquartered in Rotterdam and London. It's one of the oldest and largest companies in the world and its household brands, like Dove, Axe, Knorr, Magnum, and Domestos, are available in around 190 countries.

Unilever also has one of the most established and respected management trainee programmes for young people who want to forge a career in marketing. As a result, this scheme is highly competitive. I succeeded in joining it in the autumn of 1988, working for Birds Eye Wall's, one of its operating companies at the time, and I was pretty proud of my achievement. So was my Winner gene.

My career roadmap over the next 10 years was now neatly laid out in front of me and the future seemed bright. Trainee to brand manager to marketing manager to marketing director. Easy as 1, 2, 3.

The first few days, weeks, and months were all fairly uneventful. I was a marketing trainee going through a series of job rotations, interspersed with residential training courses every few months or so. I was part of a cohort of other new joiners dabbling in the world of big business for the first time. Nobody was under any great pressure to perform, no big expectations placed on us. I was on a steep learning curve and most mistakes were quickly forgiven.

During this period, there wasn't sufficient evidence to help decide whether I had landed the right job or not, or whether it suited my genetic make-up. To be honest, it was probably too early to be asking myself that kind of question anyway. I was working for Unilever, one of the most prestigious companies in the world, receiving the best early career development I could possibly ask for. That was surely enough.

So, head down and just get on with it.

I did just that and the early feedback I received from my line managers was all very positive. I was heading in the right direction.

Twelve months later, I found myself pacing up and down the basement of the Birds Eye Wall's building in Walton-on-Thames liked a caged animal. I was alone, surrounded only by freezers full of frozen beef burgers and fish fingers and my own confused thoughts. I was trying to work out why I was suddenly feeling so anxious, why I seemed incapable of completing the most basic of tasks at my desk upstairs. I just needed a bit of head space, away from people, to think clearly and try to work out what on earth was going on in my frazzled mind. I wasn't swamped by major decisions or weighed down under huge amounts of work pressure or imminent deadlines. I was only a trainee, the lowest of the low. Admittedly, as time had passed, I was handed a little more responsibility and people in the team were relying on me to get things done. But I was still a relatively insignificant cog in the wheel.

I didn't know it at the time, but I was experiencing my first little blip.

A couple of weeks earlier, I had started fretting over every small decision, and with the increased fretting came further indecision. The more indecisive I became, the less productive I was. And the less productive I was, the longer it took me to work my way through the to-do list for the day.

The pressure was gradually building.

I vividly remember one of my responsibilities at this time: to ensure all the copy on the packaging was completely accurate before thousands upon thousands of packs were printed. It was a thankless job requiring me to dive into the detail. I had to check every letter in every word in every line. I always dreaded the call from some wise guy on the production line asking, with just a hint of mischief, whether the company was really selling "beef buggers" instead of "beef burgers". There were significant costs associated with that kind of mistake. So, I would check, re-check and check again.

One day, I looked at that to-do list of mine and found myself incapable of doing anything on it. I froze. That's when the basement wandering started.

I had absolutely no idea what was happening to me. This had all come on very quickly, with no obvious warning signs. It had snuck in stealthily underneath the radar and I became very fearful of the events that were slowly unfolding. It was a very uncomfortable and unpleasant sensation I had never experienced before.

MARK HAD FOUND SOMEWHERE
QUIET TO TRY AND WORK OUT
WHAT WAS HAPPENING TO HIM

At this time, I was living with my younger brother, Michael, a trainee accountant with Price Waterhouse, and we were sharing a two-bedroom flat in Wimbledon. As I sat on the stairs in our flat at midnight, staring into space, unable to sleep or articulate how I was feeling, he remained worried and helpless. Caring for a brother who seemed to have lost the plot wasn't really his expertise.

Mel and I had now been going out together for just over three years. We had met in our first job after leaving university, working at a company called Ocean Transport and Trading. Throughout this entire episode, I remember her being perplexed more than anything else. Neither she nor my brother were quite sure what to say or do. It all felt a bit "out of the blue", especially for me.

After a few days of dithering, procrastinating, and increased suffering, my to-do list was growing longer and longer, and I knew it would only be a matter of time before my colleagues began suspecting that something was very wrong. I considered approaching HR but was worried, quite irrationally, that any admission of mental weakness would be the death knell of my Unilever career. Even though I was in a very junior position with not too much at stake, it still felt like a very competitive workplace.

In any case, what would I say to them? How would I explain what I was thinking and feeling when I wasn't even sure myself?

Finally, I bit the bullet and decided to confide in my boss. It would have been the last thing he wanted to hear. He was an extremely well-organised and productive professional but still had more than enough on his plate as it was. But mercifully, and without any hesitation, he told me to take a week off, get some help, and to come back when I was feeling better. I'm sure he knew what had happened to me, but he promised not to mention this to anyone else, treat it as if it were no big deal. That bought me some welcome breathing space.

During my week off work, I went to see a doctor who told me that I'd simply had a panic attack, nothing more serious. He prescribed me some medication for a few weeks and sent me on my way. I went back to work a week later, things improved, but my enjoyment levels remained depressingly low. And that was that, for now.

Years later, when I experienced my "Big Blip", I found out from the psychiatrist treating me at the time that the correct medical term for my little blip was a condition called agitated depression. Although many people experience symptoms such as feeling slowed down and lethargic when they are depressed, others may experience just the opposite. They may feel anything from fear and agitation to irritability and anger.

I felt frightened and agitated all the time.

Stuttering and Stumbling On

It is fair to say I proceeded to stumble my way through the next four years at Unilever, never being completely comfortable in what I was doing, never performing at my best, always slightly anxious. It was gradually dawning on me that I wasn't destined for the higher echelons of the company. I certainly wasn't fast-track material.

Although I did reach the first step on the corporate ladder at the end of the training scheme when I was promoted to a brand manager, I couldn't ever claim to be a natural in this role. Mental health wise, nothing dramatic happened during this period, and there were no more panic attacks or basement wandering. But there were plenty of Sunday evening blues and car journeys to work I wished would never end.

During this time, I also decided to try transcendental meditation as a way of reducing the stress and anxiety levels that were building up. I had become a bit of a sucker for "self-help" books in my quest for continual personal development and many of them were now promoting the benefits of meditation. This was the fashionable preventative "medication" of the time. The approach had also been strongly recommended by my mother who was using it to keep her own anxiety at bay.

So, twice a day, morning and evening, I would sit somewhere comfortable, close my eyes and repeat my unique mantra silently for 20 minutes, breathing slowly in and then out. Over time, it was meant to bring peace and tranquillity to my turbulent mind. But whenever I practised the technique first thing, shortly after waking up, my head was crammed so full of the jobs to be done for the day ahead that there was simply no space for the mantra to be heard. It was bullied out of the way by more dominating work thoughts. And when I got back home and practised it for a second time in the early evening, I was so mentally exhausted from the stresses and strains of the previous 10 hours that I would quickly fall asleep after five or six repetitions of the mantra.

I wasn't doing transcendental meditation any justice at all. The stress of work was putting it under too much pressure to work its magic on me.

The root problem, however, was I had found myself in the wrong job.

As a brand manager, I was often at the centre of things, continually involved in decision-making, day in and day out. *What's your view on this? Or that? This pantone colour, or this one? A small beef burger, or a larger one? TV campaign or press advertising? £2 million budget or £3 million?* This position of responsibility and the constant need to make judgement calls were pure paradise to my peers, but not to me. There was too much uncertainty, too much grey, not enough black and white. And there was no time to sit back and reflect.

I was now approaching my 30th birthday and had hobbled my way through my career like a man on crutches, striving hard to keep up but slowly falling behind. It had been painful, and the 10-year roadmap was already in tatters. Unfortunately, I was discovering a harsh lesson in life. Progression wasn't as simple or as straightforward as the 1, 2, 3 I had thought when I'd first started this journey. My Worry gene was beginning to buckle under all the stress, my Winner gene was beginning to wonder why I wasn't winning, complaining that all my peers were overtaking me. Small cracks were beginning to appear in my mental armour.

My early- to late-twenties will always have a little black mark against them because of this. For large chunks of time, I didn't really enjoy the 10 hours I spent at work every day, every week, and every year. As a result, it became quite difficult to fully embrace other aspects of my life. No matter how much I had going for me on the personal front, I found my love of life was tainted by the fact I was unhappy for much of the time on the professional front.

To be honest, I really had nothing much to complain about. Mel was a wonderful partner, we were blessed with great sets of friends, and we had enough disposable income to enjoy London life to the full. But looking back at this time, I would probably only award it a 6 out of 10. There was definite room for improvement. The job was to blame for the low score.

No, that's not accurate. The job wasn't to blame. Brand management in Unilever is a great job. Just not a great one for me.

I was a square peg in a round hole.

The Secret to Life

I think I have worked out the secret to a happy life. It involves numbers (hear me out!). There are 24 hours in a day. Let's assume you sleep for eight hours, work for eight hours, and relax for eight hours. Therefore, if you end up with a partner, we can safely assume that the combined time spent at work and with your partner probably accounts for not far off 100% of the total time available.

So, this is the secret.

As long as you are blessed with good health and a bit of luck, the route to happiness is firstly picking the right life partner, secondly, choosing the right career, and then sticking with both. The sooner, the better.

If you're more into words than numbers, Mother Teresa validates the second part of the equation by saying that 'work without love is slavery'.[4] Leo Christopher, poet and author, validates the first part with this thought: 'There's only one thing more precious than our time and that's who we spend it on'.[5]

After a courtship lasting almost six years, Mel agreed to marry me on a sunny afternoon in Ascot, Berkshire on 30th May 1992. During our period of dating, Mel had borne witness to my little blip at Unilever, but I think she accepted this as part and parcel of being in your twenties. Everybody our age was still trying to find their feet, establish who they were and decide what they wanted out of life. Fortunately for me, nothing I did or said during that time made her hesitate when I eventually popped the question.

Twenty-five years later, I can say without a shadow of doubt this was the smartest move of my life. Mel is weirdly normal. She doesn't do dramatic ups and downs, and in many ways, she is my polar opposite, the calm mill pond to my choppy waters. In the years ahead, the mental disorders of my mother, my daughter, and me would sorely test her cheerful character, but without her straightforward common sense, the endings could have been quite different.

I had found the right partner, but I was still looking for the right career.

Striking Gold

It was at the beginning of 1991 when I had a eureka moment that would change my professional life forever. I was attending one of Unilever's excellent residential training programmes, taking part in a group exercise. My group chose me to present back our recommendations to the guest lecturer in front of the rest of the class. You'd have thought that my Worry gene would have found this stressful, but actually, I enjoyed the entire experience.

At the end of the session, the lecturer awarded a white and black branded T-shirt to the person he felt had made the most

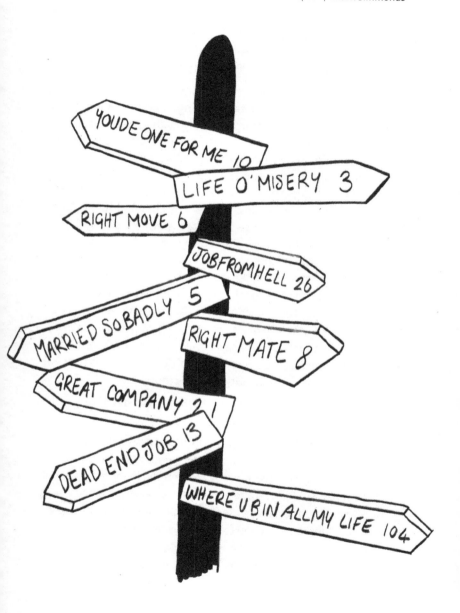

impactful presentation. That person turned out to be me. It wasn't a particularly big achievement in the grand scheme of things, but I was quietly chuffed. Maybe I wasn't the best marketer in the room, but on that day, I was deemed to be the best presenter.

It was at this point that I realised I was fishing in the wrong pond. I should really have been working in an educational role, where interacting and communicating with others were key. Interestingly, the part-time jobs I had enjoyed most when I was a student were working in schools that taught English as a foreign language, both in London and on the South Coast. I loved these jobs with a passion and was also good at them. So, the question I was now asking myself was why I had found myself so far off-course. Why had I chosen a career path so removed from the kind of work that really floated my boat and which totally energised me? Was it the pressure I placed on myself to get a well-paid corporate job rather than exist on a meagre teacher's salary, or was I trying to meet the imagined expectations of my parents and "pay them back" for the time and money they had invested in me? After all, I had emerged from a top university with a 2:1 degree and my CV was saying all the right kinds of things. Everything seemed to be directing me down the conventional route, a career either in the City or in Big Industry.

Whatever my reasoning, in hindsight, it had been very poor and narrow thinking on my part.

But right now, I was just plain tired of sticking to what was "conventional". For the next 12 months, I embarked on a journey to find the job that was right for me. Something in the educational space where I could leverage the commercial experience I had gained working at Unilever. And even though I would have to face up to countless rejections, numerous dead-ends, and plenty of disappointment, the fact I knew roughly where I was heading meant my stress levels subsided. During this period, I was like a dog that wouldn't let go of a bone. I now had a clear destination and I was going to do everything necessary to reach it.

One of the core character traits I've always been proud of is my ability to "bang a hard left", to take a completely new direction if I felt it was the right one to take. Work became slightly more bearable back in 1992 because "banging a hard left" meant there was now light at the end of the tunnel.

I was just desperate to reach it.

CHAPTER 3

FINDING AND LOSING YOUR MOJO

It was a cold, wet morning in the first week of January 1993.

I was now 31 years old. Mel and I had got married the year before and we would have our first son, Will, a year later.

Four weeks previously, I had been working for Unilever, surrounded by bright and motivated people. I had all the perks you could wish for. Pension scheme, career development, worldwide travel, training, personal mentors. On paper, it seemed an absurd thing to do, but I left this land of promise and opportunity towards the end of 1992, as much for my sanity as anything else. It was a great company, and for the rest of my working life I would always start off any conversation about my career with a proud "My first few years were spent in brand management at Unilever ..."

However, at that point in my life, Unilever was not for me. It was hurting too much.

Paradise Found

I had just started a new job as a marketing trainer, working for a company called The Management Training Partnership (MTP) in "downtown" Aylesbury. I was on my own in the board room / meeting room / "somewhere quiet to work" room. There were only 20 other people or so employed by the company. Very few were in the office that day. In fact, very few had been in the office all week. There was no pension in place, no formal training, no clear career progression, no frills, no spills. The company only turned over a couple of million or so and had been going for just seven or eight years.

But MTP was pure heaven to me. I was in my element. The cat had finally got the cream.

I had joined a very small training company which designed, developed, and delivered training courses in finance, marketing, and interpersonal skills for a number of large global companies across the world, including, somewhat ironically, Unilever.

The reason I was so happy for the first time since leaving university was that I had finally found the perfect job for me. One that made me leap out of bed every morning. One I didn't mind putting in extra time for, and one that brought a big smile to my face whenever I talked about it with my friends. And most important of all, it was the job that for several years would keep my Worry and Winner genes as happy as pigs in mud.

When I tried to identify the drivers underpinning my newly discovered joy, I located two.

The first was the satisfaction I got from helping others develop and learn. I was more of a "people person" than a "task person", and this would remain my core motivational driver for the rest of my professional career.

When working as a brand manager, the main job objective is to grow brands profitably, and to do this you need to design great products, develop impactful advertising, produce detailed business plans etc. Your focus is always on tasks and getting "things" done. Yes, you work with or through people to achieve this, and the more senior your position, the more people-oriented your role becomes. But fundamentally, you are there to make profit and keep the shareholders happy.

By contrast, when working as a trainer at MTP, your product is the people. Your goal is to help a group of willing (and sometimes unwilling) participants change the way they think about something by connecting with them on a human and interpersonal level. What gave me enormous fulfilment was seeing people learn, have fun doing so, and then go on to do things differently as a result.

The second reason for my joy was that even though I liked helping others, I was really a closet introvert. Introverts like to recharge their batteries by spending time alone and they tend to lose energy from being around people for long periods. Warren Buffett, Bill Gates, J.K Rowling, Barack Obama, and Meryl Streep are all self-confessed introverts.[6] Introverts often work slowly and deliberately. They like to focus on one task at a time and can have impressive powers of concentration. They are also very happy to let their minds hibernate a little and wander a lot.

Extroverts, on the other hand, gain their energy from others and can find this energy diminishing when they spend too much time alone. They recharge by being social and often find being by themselves more exhausting than being with others. Muhammed Ali, Bill Clinton, Margaret Thatcher, Winston Churchill, and Beyoncé are all famous extroverts.[7] They tend to tackle assignments quickly, make fast decisions, and are comfortable multi-tasking and risk-taking. They love the buzz of a loud, busy working environment, relish seeing their diaries jam-packed with meetings, and positively purr when the corridors are congested with colleagues having conversations.

A slightly contentious statement, but I have always felt it is harder in life to be an introvert than it is to be an extrovert. Some people can think there is something not quite right with you because of the way you behave. *Why are you on your own so much? Why don't you want to come out and socialise? Why don't you contribute more to the conversation?* It's as if society only sees you as being "normal" if you are happy surrounded by humanity 24 / 7, and strangely "abnormal" if you are happy to be surrounded by nobody but yourself.

Mel is an extrovert. Her perfect weekend goes something like this: nice meal out with a big group of friends on Friday evening, drinks party on Saturday, roast lunch with the whole family on Sunday. Shopping squeezed in sometime and somewhere in between. Incessant texting and WhatsApping. Watching a period drama on Sunday evening with a glass of wine and a large pack of salt and vinegar crisps (cat and dog nearby). In bed at midnight after a final WhatsApp frenzy on one of her three girlfriend groups.

My ideal weekend is fundamentally different. Meet up with a few close friends on either a Friday or Saturday evening in local pub. Not both. Drink and chat from six until half past eight by which time my social gene is exhausted. Hours spent gardening, walking the dog, watching sport on TV, YouTubing. Alone obviously. My Sunday evening routine of choice consists of watching a one-hour documentary, followed by the *Ten O'Clock News*, and finishing off the day with a 30-minute bedtime ritual: 15 minutes in the bath listening to weird and wonderful music on the radio, another 15 minutes tucked up reading a fast-moving thriller that doesn't require too much thinking. Lights out at eleven. Heaven.

During the week Mel and I have to negotiate hard about our weekend schedule to meet our respective extrovert and introvert needs. But to be fair, without her, I would have an extremely limited social life.

Another one of my little theories is that if you enjoy being either an introvert or an extrovert at the weekend, then you should try to find a working environment during the week which feeds your natural preference. Why wouldn't you? When I was working as a brand manager in Unilever I was always the hub in a wheel full of spokes and it was very difficult to find the "me-time" I needed. I was perpetually on call and in demand. Being an introvert in a large extrovert-dominated company like Unilever caused me stress. However, as a management trainer working at MTP, the "extrovert time" I spent with people in the classroom – intense, exhilarating, and richly rewarding though it was, only worked because of the many gorgeous hours of introvert-friendly solitude I enjoyed preparing for courses, travelling to and from workshops. Bothered by nothing and nobody, my uncluttered mind felt liberated and free to be creative. The relaxed, loose and hands-off management style at the company also suited me down to the ground.

Introversion or extroversion? Task focus or people focus? Which is better? Neither. All that matters is correctly identifying your own True North and then choosing work surroundings where you can thrive. This should automatically have a positive impact on your mental health. But if you are an introvert surrounded by extroverts or if you are asked to focus on task completion when your preference is primarily people, this is always likely to put unnecessary pressure on your mental state. And obviously vice versa.

Aged 30, I had found the right job not only because my introverted nature and need for people focus were satisfied but also because my Winner and Worry genes were kept fulfilled. My Winner gene now enjoyed an environment where I performed well, received constant positive feedback from colleagues, clients, and participants, and continued to learn and earn more. Equally importantly, my Worry gene no longer had to deal with the daily stress of decision-making, being asked to make judgement calls, and having to tackle all the grey uncertainties of brand management. The world of training is more predictable, and the classroom has always been my refuge, my safe place where I feel most relaxed and in control of the situation. It was also something I could meticulously prepare for, just like in my school days.

My Worry gene liked that a lot. Bizarrely enough, it was never triggered by the pressures of either training or facilitation. I think this is because these kinds of activities required me to be instinctive, to think on my feet. I didn't stress or worry, not because I didn't care, but because there wasn't the time to overthink things or become anxious. It was for this reason I found playing golf so much more stressful than playing rugby. The minutes spent walking from one shot to the next and the seconds spent standing over the ball just before I played the shot just did my head in. My brain was bombarded by a dozen conflicting swing thoughts, one of which always was, 'For God's sake, please don't miss the ball.'

A short anecdote:

When Mel and I got married in June 1992, we went to Bali, Indonesia, for our honeymoon. At that point, I was desperate to leave a job in Unilever that wasn't for me. Exactly one year later, I was relaxing in a deckchair one Sunday evening, sipping a cold beer, watching the sun set through the palm trees. I was calmly preparing for a five-day workshop I was about to run, ironically, for Unilever's young graduates from all over the Far East. I was back on the paradise island of Bali, now doing a job I loved with a passion.

The moral of this quick diversion is this. Things can and do change, but it is up to you to make them happen. If you are unhappy with your lot, then be proactive and do something. And when things don't work out as quickly as you would like, don't give up. Persist. Keep going. Something will happen.

Steve Jobs famously said that "the only way to do great work is to love what you do. If you haven't found it, keep looking. Don't settle. As with all matters of the heart, you'll know when you find it."[8]

Because my Worry and Winner genes were kept satisfied, most of my thirties were a joyful time, both personally and professionally. When Emily was born in 1996, Will had just turned two and we were a proper little nuclear family. We had moved out of London by now and were enjoying the wide-open spaces of leafy Buckinghamshire, renting first and then buying our first home in a small village called Stewkley.

I felt no more Sunday evening blues, no wishing the week away, and no longing for Friday to come quickly. Being a marketing trainer meant I was always dealing with professionals who had escaped the stresses and strains of office life, even if it was only for a couple of days or so. As a result, they were more relaxed and easy going, happy to let their hair down and have a bit of fun. I was only too eager to provide an environment where this was possible. I travelled the globe to far-off places, meeting all kinds of interesting people, learning loads along the way, laughing lots, and earning enough. After five years of working there, I was promoted to become a director of the company. I think it's safe to say, I was doing well. The beef burger freezer cabinet in the Birds Eye Wall's basement seemed a long, long time ago.

So, by all accounts, this chapter should now mark the end of a very short book.

It doesn't because life doesn't always work that way.

Paradise Lost

For many years, Johnny Walker, the famous whisky brand, was supported by the advertising strap line – "Keep Walking".[9] The underlying insight was that if you got your head down, worked hard, and persevered, you would move forward and make progress. In 2015, it was felt that the work-oriented tone of the message didn't quite resonate in the way it used to. Genuine progress and meaningful success would only arrive if the starting point was a place of contentment and optimism. So, the new tagline became "Joy will take you further. Keep walking."

My problem, as I headed towards the end of my thirties and the end of the century, was that the joy of the job had started to wane. This was affecting my joy of life.

I had stopped walking.

I slowly began to lose my mojo. The balance between introversion and extroversion remained healthy. That wasn't the problem. My desire to help people was still much stronger than my need to complete tasks. That wasn't the issue either. Unfortunately, I had taken my eye off the ball in two other key areas, and as a result, my mental barriers started to weaken.

The first area of neglect involved my Worry and Winner genes. Worry gene had been happily dormant for a number of years. He was fine. But Winner gene had become complacent, had stopped growing professionally, settling for more of the same rather than experimenting with the new. My routine began to resemble a conveyor belt in a factory, churning out the same old stuff, day in, day out, and going through the motions on automatic pilot. The same training courses, same material, same old jokes. The net effect of this inertia was that I became slightly bored by the job and increasingly frustrated. I was not putting myself in situations that would stretch me and get the adrenaline going.

Although I had climbed the ranks in my company, reaching the level of director and earning a decent wage, this was not enough to satisfy my Winner gene's hunger and need to progress up the corporate ladder. The lack of prospects in a small company fuelled my sense of dissatisfaction and drove me to start looking at alternatives. Should I leave the company and venture out on my own? Worry gene twitched nervously. Should I play safe and join a larger training establishment? Winner gene frowned disapprovingly.

The second area of neglect concerned my body and mind. My unforgiving work ethic was beginning to take its toll. It became normal to start work at eight o'clock in the morning, get home at seven in the evening, eat dinner at eight o'clock and collect emails between nine and eleven. In addition to a full working week, I would often willingly sacrifice a Sunday morning to catch up or prepare for the week that followed. My working day could only end when a comprehensive to-do list had been developed for the following day. I was driven hard by this ritual and had no chance of relaxing in the evening or at the weekend if the next day or the week ahead were not completely mapped out. It gave me a sense of satisfaction whenever I crossed off completed tasks with a triumphant swoosh of the pen. If I ever did something I hadn't put on the list, I would add it and then cross it out immediately. A retrospective swoosh.

This hectic work style was exacerbated by the fact that I was travelling abroad to far-flung places for as many as 120 days a year, often running back-to-back courses for a week or two at a time. Precious weekends had to be sacrificed and saying goodbye to the family on a Friday evening with a "see you in a couple of weeks" sigh was beginning to grate. Jet lag was also becoming less forgiving, mentally and physically, the older I got. Both body and mind were beginning to complain.

I was slowly starting to burn out and things were becoming silly.

My self-imposed and unremitting workload also had a detrimental effect on my general fitness. A youth spent playing any and every sport was replaced by a decade of inactivity and lazy armchair spectating. Although the value of exercise to mental wellbeing was not yet high on society's agenda, I should have known better. I was stuck in the era personified by Gordon Gekko and the film *Wall Street*, when lunches were for wimps and burning the midnight oil was the accepted norm. To be fair, we were still years away from busy role models like Barack Obama working out for 45 minutes, six days a week, playing golf and shooting hoops on the local basketball courts.[10] Or Oprah Winfrey keeping herself physically and mentally healthy by doing four to five strength-training sessions a week, as well as sitting in self-imposed silence for 20 minutes, twice a day.[11]

However, even back in the late 90s, a balanced life was now becoming the "new normal" in society at large. It was no longer very clever to beat your bosses into work in the morning, outlast them in the evening or send them an email just before midnight on a Saturday, copying in a whole bunch of others "just for information".

Mark Simmonds

To:	Boss
Cc:	Rest of the operating board; extended team; mum & dad; Mel's parents; a few selected friends
Subject:	10 year strategic plan

Dear Boss,

I hope you are enjoying your Saturday evening. I was at a loose end, so I thought I would start working on the 10 year strategic plan. No time like the present, as they say! See attached. A hard copy will be on your desk first thing on Monday. I will be in at 7.30am as usual.

Enjoy the rest of the weekend!

Best wishes,

Mark

P.S. Send my regards to your lovely wife.

Mark Simmonds

Unfortunately, I didn't get that memo.

Without knowing it, I was now entering dangerous territory. Worry and Winner were struggling for different reasons. My body and mind had not been particularly well looked after and there were all the makings of a perfect storm. An unhealthy climate of dissatisfaction, frustration, and impatience was starting to brew in my head, and the gathering storm clouds were leaving me more and more vulnerable.

It was now early 2000. I was 37 years old. I had been with MTP for seven years and, overall, they had been very rewarding years. I had found the right career, but that career now needed fresh impetus. It had stalled and required an urgent kickstart. The previous April, our third child, Jack, was born. Will was now five years old and Emily, three. During this time, Mel and I had divided and conquered in terms of our overall responsibilities. In part, due to my excessive travelling, she happily sacrificed her career to take on the roles of full-time mum and domestic boss, overseeing all things financial and practical. This left me as the sole bread winner in the family. The arrangement worked equally well for both of us, and we learnt to adapt to a lifestyle that meant spending over 100 nights apart every year.

(A little aside: I think Mel came to treasure her enforced independence. I swear I often witnessed clear signs she was almost looking forward to the moment I said my fond farewells and stepped out of the house. How else would you explain her cheerful whistling or that extra spring in her step on the day of my departure? I guess I should be grateful I never found the bottle of champagne cooling in the fridge.)

Our three young kids had never known anything different, but they would all understandably demand their share of "daddy time" whenever I was back in the country.

But daddy was now sick and tired of getting on and off planes. Just as I had done seven years previously, it was now time to make something happen. I needed to "bang a hard left" again.

A strong dose of something new was required to replace the mojo I had lost. That strong dose would be administered somewhat unexpectedly on a flight to New York in February of that year.

It would be a lightning bolt, completely out of the blue.

CHAPTER 4

THE CLIMB TO THE SUMMIT

There can be little doubt that human beings were not designed to spend too much time in aircraft cabins. Constipation. Bad breath. Ruined taste buds. Popping ears. Swollen legs. Blood clots. Dizziness. Dry skin. Flatulence. Increased tension, anxiety, and stress. Memory loss. These are some of the physical and mental symptoms which, according to medical research, can affect individuals flying long-haul at altitudes of 30,000 feet.[12]

Doesn't sound like much fun, does it?

For much of my thirties, however, I loved it. Although I wasn't immune to several of the unpleasant conditions listed above, my time in the air was pure gold dust to me. Client-paid business trips to the Far East and the Americas had been sacred pockets of peace and calm. My mind always seemed able to de-clutter itself quickly and remained as clear as a bell as soon as I was above the clouds. The eight, nine, ten or more hours of "me-time" available, uninterrupted by emails pinging into my inbox, presented me with a unique opportunity to do much of my "big thinking". With an absence of hustle and bustle, my Worry gene felt wonderfully relaxed, allowing my creative juices to flow freely for the duration of the trip.

An introvert's paradise.

The Birth of a Big Idea

It was in this land of hope and possibility that I was flying with my Unilever client, Andy Bird, to the US to try to persuade the Americans to embrace the company's flagship foundation training programme for marketing graduates.

It was February 2000.

I had been working intensively with Andy for about two years. He was a very bright and gifted individual. A first-class honours degree from Oxford was backed up by an impressive track record working for Unilever in the UK, India, and Singapore in a variety of strategic brand marketing roles over a number of years. His latest position was Vice President of Unilever's Global Marketing

Academy where he had spent the last four years setting up the function that was driving the development of Unilever's corporate marketing capabilities. This was a ground-breaking initiative which he had been handpicked to lead. Andy was a class act who seemed to make everything look easy. On top of all that, he was a personable guy with whom I had a lot in common.

We had both reached that "so now what ...?" stage in our respective careers, and we then got talking about important stuff ...

Helped partly by the courage of drink and the clarity of altitude, we started mulling over our respective plans for the future. For some time now, I had been looking to leave MTP, the training company, where I'd spent the last eight years but where I had now reached a ceiling. I had become frustrated by the lack of prospects going forward and had been suffering from itchy feet for a couple of years.

Having made a great success of his role as head of the Marketing Academy, Andy was also looking for his next move in the training / learning / capability arena.

After a few tentative "how abouts" and "what ifs", we gently nudged our way towards the exciting possibility of going into business together. The Big Idea was to combine best practice in brand marketing with leading edge learning in order to improve the skills of managers working in large organisations. It seemed an obvious idea when we added up our respective experiences and areas of expertise.

Andy also possessed a strong Winner gene, and no doubt both his and mine could scarcely believe what they were hearing.

This turned out to be a thrilling conversation that would dictate and direct the rest of our lives.

My Worry gene remained in deep hibernation throughout the trip.

When I woke up the next morning in New York, I felt a bit like a mischievous schoolboy who had said something he really shouldn't have. The night before, we had engaged in a "big" conversation that could have serious consequences. Very sensibly, Andy and I both agreed to sleep on the idea for a couple of days, let it germinate, giving us both time and space to find out whether the gins and tonics had clouded our better judgement. I was convinced they hadn't. At least that's what my Winner gene kept whispering loudly in my ear.

A few days later, when we got in touch back in the UK, we still thought it was a great idea. During the call, Andy mentioned that for some time he had been working with somebody he rated very highly, another independent consultant called Mhairi McEwan. Mhairi had also started her career at Unilever, where she spent 13 years rising through the marketing ranks, working in the UK, France, and Egypt. She then became Vice President Marketing (Europe) for Pepsico International and Walkers Foods before becoming a highly successful consultant working for the likes of Unilever, Diageo, and Burger King. Mhairi was very likeable, extremely commercial and, as it turned out, well connected in the business world. Another class act.

Since our trip to the US, Andy had contacted Mhairi to gauge her interest, and she was really excited by the potential of the idea.

Things Start to Come Together

We suggested meeting at the Runnymede Hotel in Egham to introduce ourselves properly, discuss the new business idea in greater depth and work out how we could make this all happen.

The name "Runnymede", from which the hotel gets its name, is derived from the Anglo-Saxon *runieg* (regular meeting) and *mede* (mead or meadow), describing a place in the meadows used to hold regular meetings. It is where the Magna Carta was sealed by King John in 1215.[13] Although Andy, Mhairi, and I were not going to sign or seal anything that day, a momentous, life-changing opportunity for all of us would remain on the table.

When I left the building, two electrifying hours later, my head was spinning. By the end of the meeting, the new idea was quickly gaining weight and momentum. As Victor Hugo, the French poet and novelist, famously said, "An invasion of armies can be resisted, but not an idea whose time has come."[14] The company was going to concentrate on the area of marketing capability development. Not consultancy where solutions were provided on a plate for clients. Not simply training either, which was too narrow a focus. Our corporate mission at launch was to help marketers become better at their jobs by developing processes, tools, terminology, and a range of learning interventions, tailored to the organisations they worked for. This would ensure they received the development they required and that the marketing function would remain at the centre of the corporate map.

The power of that initial idea, the foundation upon which the business grew quickly, was such that 17 years later the company we named Brand Learning would be purchased by Accenture for many millions of pounds.

From a personal point of view, I saw this venture as the perfect opportunity to explore different facets of the learning agenda and broaden my professional horizons. At long last, I would be able to wean myself off the treadmill of foreign travel and take on the responsibility of mentoring, coaching, and guiding others instead. I found that vision of the future very enticing.

The die was cast. My Winner gene felt it had won the lottery. My Worry gene was still in deep hibernation, out for the count. And this was the problem. Little was I to know that things were going to get very interesting from now on and my mental reserves and emotional resilience would be tested like never before.

So even though the company was not legally set up until July, to all intents and purposes, the wheels were in motion the moment each of us stepped outside the Runnymede Hotel that day.

It was action stations from that point onwards.

An Absence of Due Diligence

When I reflect back on that first meeting and the weeks that followed, it wasn't so much what I did or said, but it was more the questions I didn't ask that planted the seeds of my near destruction. With the benefit of hindsight, I now realise I failed to carry out any due diligence on myself. On the verge of making the most important decision of my professional career to date, I was making it practically blind.

Unknowingly, I was putting my mental health back on the line.

Some of the questions I should have asked myself:

Do I have the skill set required to set up a business? Do I have similar values to both Andy and Mhairi? Is there sufficient chemistry between us? Do we share the same vision of what success looks like? Where do we all picture the business being in five years' time? How important is money to us all? Are we all equally ambitious? What are we prepared to sacrifice personally?

These were the precautions you might expect any individual to take before embarking on a long-term commitment. I didn't know the answers to any of those questions at the time because I didn't ask them with any real conviction. Even if I had, the idea was so exciting that I doubt I would have listened to my responses anyway. I had reached a point in my career where this was the "obvious" next step, where running my own company would be clear proof that I had reached the summit.

My Winner gene was adamant about this.

The only potential fly in the ointment was that the three of us didn't really know each other very well before embarking on our little adventure. Yes, I had worked closely with Andy in a professional context as a supplier to Unilever and Mhairi had also worked with Andy in the same vein, but I had never once met Mhairi before that meeting at the Runnymede Hotel. Even though we did all we could to get to know one another properly during our short "courting period", there would always be some inherent risks associated with our partnership in waiting. An insufficient history of shared experiences meant we didn't have the luxury of having spent any time together as a unit in the corporate trenches.

But I suppose it's a bit like marriage. You can date somebody for three weeks or three years before deciding to tie the knot. There is no guarantee that either scenario will lead to a long, happy, and prosperous marriage.

There is always some element of luck in any relationship.

A couple of frustrating years at MTP had convinced me this was the path to take. And even though I was on a decent salary and we had three young children who were becoming more and more expensive with every passing year, my blinkers were firmly in place. My mind was made up. I don't remember ever asking anybody to play devil's advocate and give me five good reasons why I should stick and play safe, including Mel. She had sensed the growing feeling of disenchantment with my current situation and the opportunity presenting itself seemed too good to miss. Working side-by-side with Andy and Mhairi, two consummate professionals, appeared to be the perfect way to re-ignite my passion for work.

Like me, Mel wasn't an inherent risk-taker in life, but even she was prepared to take the gamble.

The little Unilever blip had happened almost 10 years previously and was now but a dim and distant memory. Neither of us gave it a moment's thought. In any case, I was passionate about capability development, training, and learning in a way that I had never been about the world of brand management. You don't get blips by doing things you enjoy.

All I knew was my Winner gene remained euphoric. I was over-dosed on excitement, hope, and possibility. This wasn't the time to be sensible. I was on the verge of setting up a business with two highly talented people in a profession I loved, and the garden was rosy. Everything looked hugely promising.

And whenever my Worry gene posed a nervous question or two, Winner gene would snap back immediately, with some irritation in his voice, 'Look, if things don't work out, we can go back and get a "proper" job. No big deal. Just relax. In any case, what can possibly go wrong?'

I resigned from my company a month or so later. During my notice period, all my mental energy was channelled towards the new adventure, and the three of us were soon up and running at full pelt.

All systems were go. It was game on.

CHAPTER 5

DRIP, DRIP, DRIP, DRIP

The process of a mental breakdown is rather like Chinese water torture. You start off not feeling very much pain. Little things begin to irritate and apply pressure in different places. Drip ... Nothing significant, nothing too painful, but persistent nonetheless. Drip ... drip ... Soldier on, this will pass. Pressure builds, bit by bit. Drip ... drip ... drip ... Things become more and more uncomfortable. You now feel trapped and slightly claustrophobic. Drip ... drip ... drip ... drip ... More pressure. Is it imagined or is it real? Doesn't matter, either way you still feel trapped. Then one day, without warning, the flood gates open.

Chinese water torture is an effective method for inflicting maximum suffering because its point of focus is the brain.

A Promising Start to the New Business

In those first few months after the Runnymede meeting in April, the three of us would meet regularly to discuss, debate, and agree the strategic direction the new business would take. *Which companies are we going to target? How will we position ourselves in the market and differentiate our offering from the competition? How are we going to price our services? Will we take on full-time employees or use freelance consultants? How much should we pay them and ourselves?* All the usual hurdles any new company would need to clear before it got going.

Ironically, the company name turned out to be one of the easiest things to pick: Brand Learning. It seemed to embody our positioning perfectly.

The company, which would initially operate out of Mhairi's fully equipped home office, was officially founded and incorporated in July 2000. The three of us were equal shareholders. Exciting stuff.

By the time we started trading in November, contracts were in place with large global companies like Unilever and Diageo that already stacked up to £500,000 for the year ahead.

The business plan had been agreed, and Mhairi and Andy, using their extensive network, were pulling in new work left, right, and centre. A wonderfully calm and efficient personal assistant was recruited at the end of 2000 and we were soon to be joined by a number of other talented consultants and employees.

Brand Learning was already a proper little company going from strength to strength.

A Big Mistake Choosing Who Does What

From the word go we needed to agree who did what as far as the running and management of the company was concerned. Who would look after the administration and the back office? Who would manage the finances? Who would sort out the legal stuff? Who would establish human resource policies? Which of us was best qualified to drive the development of the website and the marketing collateral?

The workload needed to be shared out equally between the three of us.

In a moment of madness, I offered to take on the job of working alongside our professional advisers to manage our accounts and look after our legal affairs as Company Secretary. In hindsight, this was a big mistake. A big, *big* mistake. Although I was comfortable with the theory of the balance sheet, cash flow, and profit and loss statement, the responsibility of overseeing the finances for the fast-growing business would prove to be one of the straws that broke this camel's back. Numbers, numbers, numbers.

I remember working very closely with Bolton Colby, our accountants at the time. Even though they were extremely patient and did their level best to help me navigate my way through the maze of Excel spreadsheets and put various systems in place, the finance function was not my natural habitat.

The legal stuff wasn't much better. Memorandum and Articles of Association, Service Agreements, Event of Default, Option Period, Transfer Terms. All I remember from my stint as a "trainee lawyer" was trying to make some sense of these alien terms and phrases, deciphering a language that never seemed to be written in plain English. Even though it was basic contractual stuff, and even though my "hand was being held" by the experts, it was still mumbo jumbo to me.

IF ONLY MARK HAD PICKED
6, 8 AND 9

One of my most important duties during the set-up of our company was leading the development of the Shareholders' Agreement, a document that laid out the various intricacies around share ownership. Much of this focused on what would happen if one of the shareholders were to leave the business prematurely, what would happen to their shares, and how those shares would then be valued.

Ironically, many years later, that very same document would emerge from the shadows of my attic with a very painful sting in its tail.

No doubt about it, I had jumped into two of the wrong ponds. I was a concepts and clouds type, much more into the touchy feely, the warm and cuddly, and here I was volunteering to take charge of two areas of business that were the complete opposite, the crunchy and the clinical. Back in my early thirties, I had already established I was a "people focus" rather than a "task completion" kind of guy. My short stint in brand management at Unilever had taught me that valuable lesson. And the mojo I had re-discovered when I kick-started my training career at MTP had reconfirmed this.

What was I thinking?

The Pressure Starts to Build

Drip.

We were coming towards the end of 2000. The planning period for the new company had taken place between the Runnymede meeting in April and November 1st when we officially began trading. During that time, I had also been working out my notice period at MTP, the company I was leaving behind. I didn't have the luxury of any gardening leave or a two-week holiday in the sun to recharge the batteries. It was straight in. By the time we kicked things off, I have to admit I was pretty knackered.

Mhairi, Andy, and I now had our day jobs and our night jobs. My day job was a marketing trainer. I was still travelling to the US and Japan, running five-day workshops and still spending weeks away from home. I had been globetrotting for the last nine years and the glamour of foreign travel had gradually worn off. An Inter-Continental hotel looks more or less the same in New York as it does in Tokyo or Jakarta. And airports are airports the world over. I felt stale and washed-out. And although the luxury of client-paid business class travel was always a bonus, this ring-fenced time for creative thinking, watching films, and dozing off to sleep had now sadly given way to checking financial spreadsheets and proofreading legal documents. That became my night job.

Drip, drip.

When starting your own business, you quickly realise how much you miss the things you took for granted when employed in a larger organisation with more resources. In that cosy and protected environment, you are blessed with assistants to help you prepare presentations and sort out travel arrangements: the IT team are only ever one relieving phone call away; the Finance department are always on hand to process your expenses and pay you on time; a PA is there to organise your diary. These luxuries were no longer available to me. It was now do-it-yourself.

Along with my two partners, I spent a painful day finding out all I needed to know about Excel to improve the book-keeping skills I required to carry out my financial role. And the task of developing my non-existent capabilities in PowerPoint became an immediate "must learn item" on my ever growing to-do list.

Accountant. Lawyer. Microsoft Office expert. Secretary. International management trainer. I was your five-in-one. A colourful combination.

Although each of these "jobs" didn't present insurmountable challenges on their own, it was tackling them all at the same time that caused me mental anguish. As far as my Worry gene was concerned, there was too much uncertainty, too many things I was trying to get my head around at once, too many new things to master at the same time. The only time it stopped worrying was when I stepped into the training room in either London, New York, or Tokyo. That always remained my sanctuary.

Drip, drip, drip.

All of the above became very challenging in combination, and none of it was particularly enjoyable, I must confess.

And the pressure I placed on myself to keep up with Andy and Mhairi, who both seemed to be coping effortlessly with their equally heavy workloads, only served to raise my stress levels. They made everything look so easy while I felt like I was drowning.

The final drip that kept dropping on my head was that the exit from my previous company had been a tricky one. I was now working in direct competition with MTP and my departure after eight years of loyal service never sat that easily on my conscience. After all, they had given me my big career break when I had turned just 30. I would always be greatly indebted to them for that.

Drip, drip, drip, drip.

The first 10 months since the Runnymede meeting had been an exciting ride, but they had also begun to take their toll on me both physically and mentally. The travelling abroad had worn me out, the numbers and legal mumbo jumbo were proving a handful, as was Microsoft Office. I felt guilty about my former employers and under pressure to be as efficient and effective as my new business partners. My genetic make-up was starting to moan and groan.

Although my Winner gene was huffing and puffing, he was still insistent that this discomfort was the price of success. His favourite saying was, 'You're not an entrepreneur until you have had your first breakdown.' Sixteen years on, he would have quoted from the Gallup Wellbeing Index which states that 45% of entrepreneurs report being stressed, and from another survey, 30% are identified as depressed. And the final proof, if required, that I was doing the right thing, was that 23% have a family history of mental health conditions.[15]

'Mark, all the facts are firmly in your favour and your destiny is written in your DNA,' Winner gene told me.

Worry gene was becoming more and more flustered. Suddenly, he was starting to wear those "I told you so" looks and that "maybe I should have been properly consulted when we embarked on this little venture" expression. Small cracks were starting to appear. Sleeping badly, eating less, worrying more, laughing rarely. Socialising with friends had been put on the back burner, and any kind of stress-reducing physical activity had become a long-forgotten luxury.

The Beginning of the End

It was February 2001, and I was beginning to struggle.

Drip, drip, drip, drip, drip.

A side effect of my deteriorating state was that I became less and less decisive. Decisions that should have been straightforward were suddenly difficult to make, and everything seemed to take longer to process and complete. It felt as if my head was crammed full of so much information with so many pressing jobs to be done that my mental machinery was starting to seize up.

Suddenly, I was having menacing flashbacks to my time spent in the basement at Birds Eye Wall's which had taken place 10 years previously. The symptoms were worryingly familiar. Confusion, moments of fear, little signs of panic, increasing levels of agitation and anxiety.

Just under 12 months after my life-changing trip to the US with Andy, I was back on the same route to New York to run another five-day workshop. This time I didn't feel quite so liberated by the magical effect of altitude.

Hypoxia is a condition in which the body or a region of the body is deprived of adequate oxygen supply at the tissue level.[16] It is thought to be the reason why people become emotional when watching sentimental movies mid-flight.

I was sitting at a window seat, staring out of it so that nobody could see I was crying. And I was crying because I was really frightened. I was really frightened because I was unsure whether I had the right kind of visa to enter the US. I was terrified of being denied entry and having to return to the UK. How could I explain that to the client? To Andy and Mhairi?

The tears, the fears, and the terror were very real, but they were also completely out of proportion with the issue at hand. The whole thing turned out to be a non-issue and I was admitted into the US without a problem, but the root cause of my extreme anxiety and stress had nothing to do with visas. What I was doing was catastrophising, or in medical jargon, experiencing a cognitive distortion. A person who catastrophises usually predicts an unfavourable outcome to an event and then decides that if this outcome does happen, the results will be disastrous. The prediction is usually totally unrealistic and 99 times out of 100, it never materialises.

Catastrophising is a symptom of extreme anxiety and depression.

I was now clinically depressed; I just didn't know it at the time. I felt as if I were slowly starting to lose my marbles. As Rita Mae Brown, the American writer said, 'The statistics on sanity are that one out of every four people is suffering from a mental illness. Look at your three best friends. If they're okay, it's you.'[17]

When I looked around at my friends it didn't seem to me that anybody else was struggling mentally …

Drip, drip, drip, drip, drip, drip.

Throughout this difficult period, I felt unable to confide in Andy and Mhairi for all the wrong reasons. In retrospect, this decision not to confess I was in trouble was a big mistake. I think there were three reasons why I found this so hard to do. Firstly, I did not know either of them very well at a personal level, and divulging something this sensitive just seemed out of the question. Secondly, I kept trying to tell myself the discomfort I was feeling was perfectly normal, only to be expected. At least, this is what my Winner gene kept insisting. Things would get easier sooner or later and I just had to ride out the storm. In any case, most of my friends were under some kind of pressure as they tried to forge ahead in their respective careers. Thirdly, I had spent the last two or three years waiting patiently for this big opportunity. I had made it happen. The last thing I was now going to do was jeopardise it by admitting to either of my partners that I was in trouble or mentally fragile. Although mental illness in the business world remains a taboo subject even in 2018, it was doubly taboo back in 2000, where there was very little guidance on what to say or do either as a sufferer, a carer, or an employer.

Not only was I feeling under increasing pressure at work, but I was also beginning to detach myself from any meaningful kind of social life. And when I did go out with friends or family, I was only ever "out" in the physical sense of the word. Mentally, I always stayed in my own little world, cogitating and ruminating. I remained distant.

It was even worse with the children. I remember apologising to Will, my eldest son, who was now six and Emily who was four, trying to explain what I was doing, why I was absent abroad so often, and why, even when I was back home, I was spending so much time locked away in my office. I promised them things would quieten down soon and that we would soon be spending much more time together. I felt terribly guilty about not being a proper dad and not being there for them.

They just looked at me blankly.

Drip, drip, drip, drip, drip, drip, drip.

My first visit to the doctor took place on the 15th February when I was prescribed 5mg of chlordiazepoxide, a treatment for anxiety disorders. The last time I'd been to see a doctor about my state of mind was back in my Unilever days. The same symptoms were beginning to align somewhat ominously, so I decided to make an appointment. It was my own decision, prompted by my Worry gene who had begun nagging me, urging me to get help as quickly as possible.

I explained to the doctor that there was really nothing to panic about and that I was just feeling a bit anxious, not sleeping terribly well. I think I was trying to convince myself as much as him that all I was doing was taking preventative measures to nip things in the bud. Better safe now than sorry later. I would be back to normal in a week or two.

I also agreed to go to the Dove Centre, a counselling unit in Aylesbury to pick up some tips and tactics on how to cope with the escalating stress. I took the pills daily, heeded the advice given, and every morning I woke up in the hope that everything would somehow be magically better.

If only.

AN ECLECTIC COLLECTION

Anti-depressants don't work for everybody and even for those people they do work for, the positive effects of any medication are often only felt after six or eight weeks.

I needed them to work right away.

Unfortunately, it was too little and far too late. The tablets and the counselling were the equivalent of trying to put out a raging fire with a child's toy watering pistol. All the structural damage had already been done to my brain.

I stumbled on for the next few weeks, just about functioning, but it wasn't any fun at all.

Then one day the floodgates opened.

CHAPTER 6

BROKEN

Somewhat ironically, a nervous breakdown has no scientific definition in any mental health professional's lexicon. Apparently, it doesn't exist. It's purely a layman's term used to describe the point when you are unable to cope with life anymore and you come to a sudden, grinding halt. A number of colourful expressions have been used to depict this state of mind: an overloaded machine that has finally blown; snapping under extreme pressure; an organ in convulsion; circuit overload; a feeling that the entire world is crashing down and you don't know how to save it; fighting a war inside your head every single day.

9th April

It was just another Monday morning when I entered my home office at around eight o'clock in the morning and attempted to start work. I sat at my desk and switched on my PC. I opened up my notebook and had a quick look at my to-do list for the day. I turned to the first item. My mind was in a frenzy and I found it impossible to focus on the one task I had begun. I tried again, but still no luck. I was unable to think straight or concentrate for more than a few seconds before my mind became distracted, invaded by the other items on my list, all screaming for my immediate attention. After 30 minutes of either staring aimlessly at my computer screen or pacing up and down my home office, desperately trying to make sense of what was happening, I decided to change tack.

Let's grab a cup of coffee. Deep breath. Nothing serious.

Twenty minutes or so later, I was back at my desk, attempting to tackle another task on the list. It wasn't a particularly challenging one, but this made no difference. I was unable to complete the job at hand.

I was starting to become more and more agitated. I knew the longer I sat there not doing anything, the less time I would have to complete everything I had to do. The pressure continued to build.

Very briefly, I managed to pull myself together, remembering what the local counselling unit had told me about coping with stress. Deep breathing was the trick. This is because when you breathe deeply, a message is automatically sent to your brain telling you to calm down and relax. An increased heart rate, fast and shallow breathing, high blood pressure: these are all symptoms of extreme anxiety which are reduced through deep breathing.

Close your eyes ... breathe in, hold your breath, breathe out ... breathe in, hold your breath, breathe out ... breathe in, hold your breath, breathe out ...

Five minutes later, I was back at my computer. No change. My mind was still racing. I got up and completed a few more circuits of the room. This time, I began to bang my head hard against the wall out of both frustration and fear. I did this several times in a futile attempt to knock some sense into myself. This wasn't happening, I told myself. This couldn't be happening.

It was now mid-morning, time was marching on, and I had been totally unproductive for about two hours. My stress levels were rising with every passing minute. Nothing had been ticked off my to-do list. Absolutely nothing.

I left my home office again and returned to the kitchen. I needed to talk to Mel who had dropped the two older children off at school. She would know what to do. I explained I had a problem. By talking slowly and calmly, I tried to normalise the situation, make out things were not as serious as they so obviously were. I wanted to feel I was still in control. Mel suggested I reduce my to-do list for the day to a couple of items only and tackle them one at a time. As usual, Mel's rational advice seemed very sound and sensible. Of course, I told myself, that was the obvious thing to do. Silly me. Take one thing at a time, get some momentum going and once you are in the groove of getting things done, you will be fine.

I returned to my office desperately trying to pretend that the little blip was just that and all would be okay on my return. But back at my desk, all was unfortunately not okay. I picked one thing to focus on just like Mel had told me. Still nothing. Mind frozen. The computer in front of me had now become a man-eating lion, not letting me get anywhere near the keyboard, roaring at me to go away and not come back.

With an escalating sense of panic, Mel and I made an emergency appointment at the doctor, where we explained the events of the morning in the context of the last couple of months. Very quickly he decided my medication needed to be reviewed but he also strongly recommended I took time off work. He suggested three weeks.

As soon as he uttered those magical words, I felt an enormous sense of relief. I knew this would have implications all round, but at long last the situation had been taken out of my hands.

The doctor re-assured me this was not unusual. I had suffered a burnout. Quite common and nothing a few weeks' rest wouldn't cure.

I made a difficult but relieved call to Andy, who was unsurprisingly shocked and sympathetic in equal measures. This had come completely out of the blue for both of my partners. Up to this point, I had been functioning normally in the eyes of the outside world. I was still getting things done.

But inside, I had obviously been close to breaking point.

Stepping Off the Treadmill

For the next three weeks, I remained at home on sick leave, under strict instructions both from the doctor and Mel not to think about work, and not to go anywhere near my home office.

I wish I could say it was a relaxing time, the much-needed break that would put me back on track, but unfortunately much of it was spent trying to come to terms with what had happened. My mind was still whirring away, day and night. It had now entered the 24-hour Le Mans race where there are no pit stops and where you just go around the same track. Time after time after time. Mel and I tried to get out a bit, pretending everything was normal, but it wasn't. We both knew it. My conversations both with her and our friends were distant and detached.

My Winner gene kept trying to persuade me, unconvincingly, this was just a small hiccup, a tiny inconvenience all budding entrepreneurs experienced. My Worry gene had started battening down the hatches, getting itself ready for an impending storm.

On Friday 27th April, I met my two partners at the end of the three-week break to decide on a way forward. We met in a restaurant to talk things over, and there was plenty of sympathy. I was very honest with them about the pressure I had been feeling. I wasn't coping, and I needed to put the brakes on for a bit. As a result, mercifully, I was relieved of my financial accountant's responsibilities.

From that point onwards, Mhairi would take control of all things financial and legal, and she proved to be much better qualified than me in both areas. And when she soon recruited an accountant with 40 years' experience, the commercial side of the business would finally be run by able professionals rather than by a willing but inexpert amateur, who was out of his depth.

So, my overall workload was reduced, and an ongoing plan of attack was agreed to help me get back on track. A return to work on Monday, and normality. Crisis averted.

Unfortunately, it didn't feel that way over the next 48 hours. The gradual build-up of pressure in my mind through Saturday and Sunday were scant evidence of a return to normality or the end of any crisis.

The Le Mans race was still going strong in my head.

Broken. Kaput. Game Over.

On Monday morning, I woke up early after a restless night's sleep. I walked into my home office a little bit like a man entering a room where he knows he won't be welcome. I opened my workbook and looked at my now much reduced to-do list. But each item still seemed like the equivalent of climbing Everest. I was praying my computer would be less hostile than it had been three weeks previously. It wasn't. Once again, my mind seized up.

No! No! No! No! No! Noooooo! Please, God, no!

More pacing up and down, more demented headbanging, more last-ditch attempts at deep breathing.

Nothing had changed. I had now broken down completely. The little blip had just become a big one. The engine had been spluttering badly for a number of months. I hadn't got it checked out when I should have, and now it had given up the ghost. A few frantic attempts to turn on the ignition had proved futile. It was stone dead.

Now here is the supreme irony.

Although a nervous breakdown is extremely frightening, it is also an essential part of the human defence system. Fundamentally, it's a good thing. If you put your hand on a very hot oven plate by accident, the moment your mind senses you will get burnt, you instinctively pull it away to avoid it getting hurt. Similarly, if you try to hold your breath underwater for a long period of time, your mind eventually orders you to re-surface when your brain is being deprived of the oxygen it needs.

When stress builds up in the mind to a point where things are becoming psychologically and physically dangerous, the brain takes matters out of your hands. It presses the emergency "stop" button and shuts you and your system down whether you like it or not. It won't restart the engine until it thinks it's safe to do so. In most cases, this takes place relatively quickly, once it's absolutely sure you are out of danger. This is what happened to me many years previously when I had suffered my panic attack at Unilever.

This time around, however, my engine would need major repair work. I didn't know it at the time, but it would remain stone dead for some time to come.

CHAPTER 7

INTO THE DARKNESS

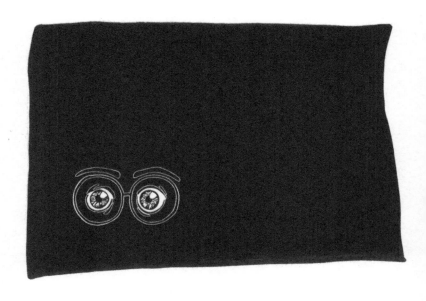

'Hope is being able to see that there is light despite all the darkness.' Desmond Tutu, South African Anglican cleric. Winner of the Nobel Prize for Peace.[18]

Picture the scene. It was 2nd May 2001. I had just taken three weeks off work to get myself back on the straight and narrow, and this had failed miserably. The period of rest and recuperation had had no effect whatsoever on my mental wellbeing. My mind was still broken. Mel and I returned to the doctor in a state of bewilderment, at a loss to understand, let alone explain, what was happening.

Without much hesitation, he recommended I take a break from work for a further unspecified period. He prescribed a new combination of anti-depressants and anti-anxiety pills. Once more, I found myself on sick leave.

I was forced to make another difficult phone call to Andy, and once again, he was very understanding. Despite being a fledgling business, both partners agreed to take the hit and pay me full salary while I was off work. Without doubt this was a huge relief, but my overriding feeling was now one of utter shock. This had all happened too quickly, and I was still reeling.

Once things started to slowly sink in, once the full enormity of recent events began to strike home, the relief of being signed off work and put out of my misery was replaced by something far more sinister. Without warning, I was knocked out flat by depression. Up until then, it had "only" been extreme stress and anxiety, but now this was accompanied by a rapid downward swing in mood.

Just a few weeks previously, I had been a partner in a thriving fledgling consultancy, earning good money, with business on the up and up. And although it was proving to be a very stressful experience, there was still everything to look forward to. Painful though it all was, at least the dream was still in reach. Now, it looked like I was losing everything: my health, my career, my happiness, my self-esteem, my confidence. They were there one minute and gone the next. There were also several practical concerns that ratcheted up the pressure.

Firstly, being the sole bread winner, it was my responsibility to provide for the family. Even though I was being paid for the next few months, what would happen if I couldn't return to work once this period ended? How would we pay the mortgage? The bills? As a husband and father, these had become my responsibilities. Mel had others, all equally important. We had struck a deal between us and now I wasn't keeping my side of the bargain.

I was letting everyone down.

Secondly, there was the issue of medical insurance. I was not covered for mental illness, to any significant degree, by our insurers. If I needed to spend an amount of time in a private hospital, we would have to fund this through our own limited savings and this could end up being a bottomless pit. Being a natural worrier, these concerns assumed dramatic proportions in my fragile mind and scary monsters started popping up all over the place. Irrational catastrophising was soon the order of the day.

During those first few days and weeks, I became more and more moronic, spending hours alone in the bedroom, staring at the ceiling, desperate for every day to end, equally desperate for every new day not to begin. I found myself trapped in mental and physical solitary confinement.

On 22nd May, six weeks into my sick leave, Andy called me suggesting we meet up to discuss how we should take things forward. I felt guilty my continued absence was putting a huge burden on the business and I am sure they wanted to resolve the situation as soon as possible. It was still very much in start-up mode, and this would have been the last thing my two partners would have wanted or needed. However, I was not in a fit state to go anywhere, speak to anybody, or think about anything. It was therefore agreed we would talk again in early July.

Mel would keep in touch sporadically with Andy over the next few weeks, but there was never anything positive to report.

The Need for Black and White

I cannot stress enough how difficult those first couple of months were, living at the bottom of this very dark hole. I felt like a spider, trapped in a bath tub, desperately trying to scale the sides as the water slowly rises, but always slipping back down again.

Ned Vizzini, the American writer, summed up the sensation of depression perfectly.[19] 'I didn't want to wake up. I was having a much better time asleep. And that's really sad. It was almost like a reverse nightmare, like when you wake up from a nightmare, you are so relieved. I woke up into a nightmare.'

Vizzini was just 32 years old when he committed suicide.

J.K Rowling has talked about her experience of depression in the following way: 'It's so difficult to describe depression to someone who's never been there, because it's not sadness. I know sadness. Sadness is to cry and feel. But it's that cold absence of feeling – that really hollowed-out feeling.'[20]

One thing is for sure, it's a relentless illness where everything remains a different shade of black for days, weeks, and months on end.

During this desperate period, I visited an army of specialists and counsellors, some recommended, and some (believe it or not) plucked randomly out of *Yellow Pages*. The problem was I did not know who to turn to, who to trust. My personality required certainty and clarity of choice, but my depressed condition could only be cured through a process of trial and error.

This was the unfortunate nature of the illness. It was grey; I wanted black or white. I wanted exactitude; it could only offer approximation.

Each of the specialists I visited had their own unique theory, their own plan for recovery. Not unreasonably, they all wanted time to work with me on a long-term basis rather than being given a couple of one-off hits. I was just impatient to get better and if I didn't sense any improvement or see any hope of progress after a couple of sessions, I would simply move on to the next expert.

It became a bit like casual dating, albeit with quite a lot more at stake. And without the fun.

It would have been so much simpler and less stressful if I had broken my leg, however badly. The process would have gone something like this: I would have seen a surgeon who would have sent me for an X-ray, assessed the damage, and decided on the appropriate treatment. Three to four months later my leg would have recovered, and life would have continued.

Curing mental illness is not so straightforward, much more hit and miss. Even in 2018, there is disagreement within the medical community about the most effective ways for treating depression. Are anti-depressants good or bad? Which of the talking therapies are the most effective? There are many points of view but little consensus.

I wanted certainty but I just couldn't get it.

Recovery proved to be elusive. Days at home were long and laborious and I tried desperately hard to keep busy. I attempted to read the paper every morning, but my brain said no. I enrolled on a course locally to try to improve my PowerPoint skills in preparation for my return to work, but my brain said no again. Anything that required mental processing of any kind remained out of bounds. Summer was approaching, and I would spend time in the garden, weeding, mowing the lawn, both on automatic pilot, engaging in mindless activities designed to occupy but not pre-occupy the brain.

My brain just about said yes to these.

There was miniscule enjoyment in anything I did. I tried to keep fit; I walked Purdey, our black Labrador, every day more slowly than a funeral march; I went shopping with Mel to escape the monotony of home. I rarely engaged with my kids like any normal father might.

A small band of close friends remained very supportive throughout this time. Always checking in with Mel or scooping up the kids for a few hours while she accompanied me to yet another consultation. Every now and then, they would come around for a coffee and chat, trying their hardest to engage me in conversation, doing their level best to normalise a situation that was very abnormal. They didn't judge or become impatient, and were always there for Mel, me, and the children. It must have been painfully difficult for them to see a good friend, now a pale shadow of his former self, and to witness the devastating effect this was having on his family.

A tiny consolation was that the illness had so far mainly coincided with the school summer term, so it was only during the evenings and at weekends that the older two, Will, aged 7 and Emily, 5, saw my suffering. Jack was a toddler at home and remained blissfully unaware of the situation unfolding around him.

Another symptom of any mental illness is that the sufferer can become increasingly introspective and more self-centred. As I deteriorated, the only person I could talk to was Mel and I became very demanding of her time. I would become irritated whenever the phone rang. The call was obviously never for me, and more often than not, it was one of our friends enquiring how I was doing and making sure Mel was coping. As soon as she put the phone down, it was back to me. My time again. Jack and I would often compete for her attention during the day. She was effectively in charge of four children and a dog, and it was me, her fourth child, who was causing her the most grief. And by quite some distance.

Mel was inspirational throughout my illness. Unlike me, she did not seem to have the slightest disposition to mental health disorders, and even though she struggled to understand initially why I couldn't just "pull myself together", she quickly learnt this "hard to fathom" illness was not a quick fix. She would have to be patient.

Mercifully, for the whole family's sake, she was very patient. For what must have seemed like an eternity, she coped with the pressure the situation was placing on her, day in, day out. She looked after the kids, played with them, always trying to shield them from the difficulties at home. She managed the house, fed us all, drove us everywhere, kept me occupied, kept me safe. She became very adept at reading the situation and playing what was in front of her. She was never sure what each day would bring, where my illness would take us next, and as a result, she wasn't able to get into any kind of predictable routine. She planned where possible but always reacted quickly whenever required.

Mel put on a masterclass in multi-tasking under extreme duress.

Trying Too Hard to Recover

Once I had been on the new medication for about a month, I was strongly advised by my psychiatrist to enrol on a couple of anti-depression courses at a private hospital in Northampton, using up some of my limited private medical insurance funding. The courses were based on an approach called cognitive behaviour therapy (CBT). In a nutshell, CBT works on the premise that mental

health can be restored and maintained through a combination of doing positive activities, thinking positive thoughts which should ultimately lead to feeling positive emotions. In that order.

The courses taught you how to plan a number of activities every day from the moment you woke up to the moment you went to bed. You would schedule in play, work, and rest in blocks of 60 minutes and you were encouraged to be as disciplined as possible. Completing the tasks was more important than enjoying them. Each week, you would become more adventurous, your levels of enjoyment would slowly rise and, little by little, you would step back into normal life.

One of the psychiatrists I turned to during my illness had a colourful way of explaining the biology of recovery. When deeply depressed, your brain is bombarded with black balls, miserable thoughts buzzing backwards and forwards. Over time, the combination of medication and therapies like CBT encourage an odd white ball of hope and happiness to appear. Eventually, the white balls start to outnumber and overpower the black ones as the shoots of recovery begin to take firm hold.

In theory, cognitive therapy made absolute sense, and I tried my hardest to fill in my daily schedule, stick to it and give white every chance of overtaking black. But mental illness doesn't make sense because it doesn't play fair. It does what it wants, when it wants.

Sometimes, the most trivial of tasks were simply beyond me. All I really wanted to do was lie on my bed, close my eyes, and go to sleep. This was the only time I was not in any pain. Unfortunately, the illness only ever granted me four or five hours' respite every night. Everything was such hard work. Even sleeping.

For me, the road to recovery had proved to be a false dawn. The anti-depression courses at the Northampton hospital had come to an end, and by this point I should have been edging back towards normality, returning to work and life as I once knew it. But I wasn't. My doctors were now scratching their collective heads, unsure which new medication to prescribe, which talking therapy to recommend next.

The white balls were nowhere in sight. The colour was still black.

I can only imagine how difficult it must have been for both my business partners during this period when they would have had so much on their plates. The cost of my absence would have caused them a real headache. The worry and uncertainty that come with any mental illness make it very tricky to deal with, to predict. I still felt very guilty that I was letting them both down badly. Guilt is often depression's partner in crime.

A few weeks into my sick leave, Andy and Mhairi needed to become more formal and procedural in their communication and correspondence with me in order to protect the interests of the business. It was now mid-June. I had been on sick leave for just over two months when I received a letter from my two partners. A 12-week sick leave period had previously been agreed and now there was the option of a further four weeks, taking this up to 30th July, if required.

Again, this was a huge relief to Mel and me from a financial point of view. Although the tone of the letter was very supportive, it was made clear that the current situation was creating financial and managerial pressures for the company and that it was in everyone's best interest to resolve what my future role would be, both "swiftly and amicably". It was suggested a meeting should be planned for early July to explore some options and decide on a way forward.

A Raging Battle Commences

I now had three weeks before I was due to meet with my partners and the clock was ticking louder and louder in my confused and crowded brain.

A violent struggle started to rage in my head between two powerful opponents, each with conflicting goals, each desperate to knock the other out. One side was called "Must Go Back", the other, "Can't Go Back". They fought furiously for three weeks, non-stop, day and night, neither prepared to give an inch of ground. "Can't Go Back" was up on points, but "Must Go Back" was putting up one hell of a fight.

As a result of this ongoing conflict, I quickly deteriorated. In moments of extreme stress, the headbanging returned with a vengeance. I am not sure what the psychological explanation for this was. Maybe it was a physical means of demonstrating my extreme mental distress. Or possibly a frantic attempt, once again, to try to knock some sense into me. Whatever it was, it was weird, and it freaked Mel out. All she could do was try to hide these bizarre behaviours from the children.

I was becoming more "bruised and bloodied" with every passing day. My brain was a war zone with no truce in sight.

The consultant psychiatrist at Isham House in Northampton, who had supervised me while I was undertaking the CBT classes, saw me at the beginning of July. This was his verdict:

He has fitful and unrefreshing sleep with quite frequent early morning waking, his mood is low, but is at its worst in the morning. He eats with no relish at all, has seriously impaired concentration with both distractibility and sluggish thinking, no real interest in anything, very little energy, and feelings of hopelessness associated with frequent suicidal thinking, but no active planning.

It was the 9th of July. The date of my planned meeting with Andy and Mhairi was fast approaching. I had made no progress. In fact, it seemed as though I had gone backwards.

As a result, I was not in a fit mental state to have any kind of coherent conversation with anyone about anything of consequence.

So Mel telephoned Andy in a state of desperation and told him I would not be able to meet with him and Mhairi as planned. Andy offered his support to Mel but mentioned that my absence was having a considerable impact on the business. He asked Mel if she could find the right moment to talk to me and ask how I wanted to proceed. He then went on to outline to her a number of broad options to facilitate my return to the business. Either I could return as a full director or return as a director with reduced responsibilities / equity. Alternatively, I could resign as a director and come back as an employee in some kind of flexible capacity when I had recovered. If I were to go for the last of these options, I would need to sell my equity back to Andy and Mhairi as per our Shareholders' Agreement.

At this time, I was barely capable of making my own breakfast, let alone making decisions that would determine my career and the rest of our lives. But I was feeling under great pressure to come to a decision, and quickly too. I had not been able to contemplate anything business-related for over three months, and the thought of discussing work, let alone returning to it – any kind of work – filled me with complete horror. I was sure the man-eating lion was still ferociously guarding my computer, though I didn't dare check. I was too ill to consider the options my two partners were putting on the table, or understand their implications.

However, during the next 24 hours, Mel and I somehow managed to talk things through. We weighed up the options as best we could, and in a futile attempt to alleviate the stress now consuming me, and in the desperate hope this might help my recovery, we finally made a very difficult decision.

I called Andy the following day. Conflicting emotions were flooding through my head. I told him I wasn't able to give him any indication of when I would be able to return to work and in what capacity.

I felt that to be fair to my partners the only option I had was to resign over the phone.

During the same conversation, we agreed we needed to reach closure on the uncertainty surrounding the business. We agreed I would be unable to operate as a director of the business. We agreed that the necessary steps would be taken to value my equity, review the implications on the business. We also agreed I would take the appropriate legal and professional advice.

We agreed rather a lot on that phone call, even though my mind was totally scrambled and confused.

A Hippocampus Under Pressure

The clinical argument for not making major decisions when suffering from a major depressive disorder (MDD) is compelling. The hippocampus, located near the centre of the brain, regulates the production of a hormone called cortisol. This is released by the body during times of mental stress and depression. Problems arise when excessive amounts of cortisol reach the brain during periods of prolonged pressure. This causes the hippocampus to shrink which in turn can lead to loss of functionality and memory problems.[21]

The prefrontal cortex is located at the front of the brain and is responsible for controlling emotions, making decisions, and forming memories. It also shrinks under extreme stress.[22]

And to complete the set, the amygdala, the part of the brain which facilitates emotional responses like pleasure and fear, becomes bigger and more active when cortisol levels increase. This results in disturbed sleep patterns.[23]

That July, mirtazapine was treating my depression, buspirone my anxiety. Zopiclone would help me get four hours' sleep a night, while olanzapine, the anti-psychotic drug, was trying to address my increasingly frenzied and erratic behaviour. Lithium carbonate was waiting in the wings just in case I turned out to be bipolar too.

DEPRESSION, DRUGS AND DECISIONS
WERE A DODGY MIX

So at the point I was making critical decisions around both employment and shareholding, my hippocampus and prefrontal cortex had both shrunk, leading to memory loss and poor decision-making; the inflated size of my amygdala meant I was completely knackered; and all parts of my poor brain were being bombarded by a powerful cocktail of drugs. Whichever way you look at things, it wasn't a great time for me to be discussing commercially complex matters or taking key decisions.

A few weeks later, I received a letter from the company confirming everything we had discussed over the phone.

Although "Must Go Back" had finally conceded, "Can't Go Back" had won what almost turned out to be a Pyrrhic victory in the days following that telephone conversation.

A dramatic sequence of events would now begin to unfold.

CHAPTER 8

END OF THE TUNNEL

Called "the perfect place to die", The Aokigahara Forest, also referred to as the Sea of Trees, sits right along the edge of Mount Fuji, roughly a two-hour drive west of Tokyo. Throughout the forest, signs have been mounted on the trees: 'Life is a precious gift', 'Quietly think once more about your parents, siblings or children', 'Please don't suffer alone, and first reach out', 'Please consult the police before you decide to die'.[24]

Since the turn of the century, up to 105 bodies have been found in the forest every year.

Experts have long considered why some choose to come to this vast forest to end their life. Three decades ago, a Japanese psychiatrist who interviewed a handful of Aokigahara suicide survivors wrote that a key reason was 'They believed that they would be able to die successfully without being noticed'.

It was 16th July 2001.

I had now been passed back into the care of the Tindal Centre, the mental health unit for adults in Aylesbury. I was seen by the Locum Staff Grade Psychiatrist. This was an extract of his letter sent to my GP:

Over the weekend, things appear to have erupted when Mr Simmonds became extremely agitated, hyperventilating and his behaviour became markedly frenzied. He started shouting at the children, stating that he believed he was the devil and that his nervous system didn't work anymore. He tried to test this by stabbing himself with a knife or attempting to cut himself on the arms ... He appeared to be fairly agitated and showed markedly impaired concentration with disjointed thinking and was continuously preoccupied.

Another member of the psychiatric team described my deteriorating condition to my GP as "worsening depersonalisation verging on nihilism". He almost made it sound like I was suffering from some kind of existentialist philosophy.

In layman's terms, life had become meaningless.

I had been on sick leave for almost three and a half months. My home had become a prison and I was now completely alone. One week earlier, in a state of utter desperation, I had felt compelled to resign from Brand Learning. The future was now looking bleak, making the present feel even more unbearable.

To Admit or Not to Admit, that is the Question

At the meeting with the psychiatrist, he strongly recommended I admit myself to the Tindal Centre, as an in-patient. I was becoming a real danger to myself, Mel, and the kids. Mel confessed she was now frightened having me at home. She felt unsafe and she was unsure how much longer she could cope with the situation. She was already hiding knives and anything else sharp in the home to protect both me and the family. She had been on a 24-hour vigil for a number of weeks and was now just plain exhausted.

The Tindal Centre was inhabited by patients with extreme psychological disorders and it played an extremely valuable role for society back in the day. Unfortunately, I was a very middle-class Englishman enjoying a very middle-class kind of life, and the thought of being admitted into a mental hospital just terrified me.

Mel and I went away to consider our options. In a weirdly calm manner, we drove to a small café in a neighbouring village to have a cup of coffee and consider the pros and cons of admission. We looked like a normal couple having an everyday conversation, and anybody listening in would have found it hard to believe what we were discussing. But this was the nature of the illness. It took things that were normal and it twisted them.

Although I was extremely depressed, there were still times when I could be totally lucid and talk quite coherently. This would contrast starkly with other times when the unrelenting pressure of the situation would lead to extreme, erratic, and frighteningly bizarre behaviours. Headbanging, self-stabbing, grunting.

It was almost schizophrenic.

After a lengthy debate, we finally decided against admission, but mainly for the wrong reasons. The stigma associated with places like the Tindal Centre was very strong at the time. A long stay there was not going to sit very comfortably or conveniently on my CV, and this was a frightening prospect for me now my career seemed to be in tatters.

With the benefit of hindsight, we made a very poor decision that day, but we ended up being extraordinarily lucky.

Locked Up in Solitary

I now resembled a total zombie, communicating with nobody. I was simply going through the motions. It felt like I was at the very bottom of the darkest of pits. My isolation from society was almost complete, both physically and mentally. My business colleagues were the first to be left behind, closely followed by my friends, and then my three kids. Now it was Mel's turn.

I had been sleeping alone at night for several months and every evening I would go to bed at midnight, dosed up with zopiclone, a powerful sleeping tablet. This would remain effective until four o'clock when I would wake up, unable to sleep any longer, my mind back at Le Mans. I would get out of bed and pace the room from one end to the next. Up and down, up and down, up and down. Ruminating, worrying, catastrophising. Mel would sleep in the spare room next door, door ajar, in case I decided to tiptoe downstairs looking for knives. Physically, we were apart, but now I let Mel slip out of my life emotionally too.

The summer holidays had just started, and the children were at home where they would remain for the next six weeks. Their proximity to me was adding to my suffering. My proximity to them and my strange antics were confusing them further and adding to their suffering. This wasn't how fathers were supposed to behave. I was now utterly useless, having failed my family miserably.

My huge sense of guilt was becoming unbearable. There was nowhere left to hide.

19th July 2001. About ten in the morning.

I found myself home alone when Mel took the kids to a friend to escape the mad house for a few hours. They all needed relief too. It was going to be a very long six weeks for everybody.

Many years later, Mel would own up to the guilt she felt about leaving me on my own that day.

The Only Solution Left

I was feeling suicidal. The walls had all closed in. There was no way out. Ranata Suzuki, a writer and poet, has said, 'There comes a point where you no longer care if there's light at the end of the tunnel or not. You are just sick of the tunnel.'[25]

We had a dusty Oxford Hammond Atlas of The World sitting on one of our bookshelves in the living room. I thumbed my way through it until I could find the most detailed map of the UK. I was looking for Beachy Head, a popular suicide spot on the south coast. I thought through the logistics but decided it was too far away, too complicated. In any case, how was I going to get there? I hadn't driven a car for a couple of months.

Time for plan B. I decided to cycle down towards the nearest railway line just outside Soulbury, a neighbouring village, 20 minutes away on the bike. The InterCity trains would pelt down this section of the track, travelling in excess of 100mph heading south to London or up north to Manchester and beyond.

However, once I had reached my destination, I realised there was no easy access down to the tracks. The embankment was fenced off. It was only then that I noticed a parked police car with a couple of officers inside. They appeared to be observing me, seemed to know I was up to some kind of mischief. Could this have been the illness talking? Was I simply hallucinating, becoming paranoid?

I gave up on plan B, turned around and started making my way back home, feeling desperate and confused. I still hadn't found my Aokigahara Forest. Ending my life wasn't proving to be as straightforward a task as I had imagined.

Fortunately, I had a plan C. One last plan before I would have to concede defeat, return home, face the kids and Mel. I cycled the long way home, through the local villages. On this route, there was a stretch of road where I had driven many times. A long and straight B-road where cars and lorries always drove too fast.

It was exhausting stuff. Most of the ride was uphill. I was very unfit. I was full up to the brim with medication. Contaminated with dark thoughts. And there wasn't a speeding lorry in sight. Where the hell were they? Eventually, I crawled my way into the village of Wing.

Then, at last, the moment I had been waiting for ... There it was ... Coming towards me ...

The next thing I knew, I was in the John Radcliffe specialist trauma unit in Oxford, having been involved in a collision with a 10-ton truck. I had suffered head injuries and a tension pneumothorax (collapsed lung) and had been transported to the hospital by air ambulance. It had been a first-class accident.

But suicide was obviously not meant for me.

When Mel and the kids returned home, they found a police car parked on the drive. The policemen had called round to inform her that I had been involved in a major incident. They told her quickly that I was alive, but in intensive care with serious injuries. Somewhat ironically, the psychiatric nurse supervising me at the time, was also waiting outside the house. He had arrived to see me for an appointment to check how I was doing.

The Psychology of Suicide

Suicide is a selfish act. People who attempt it are cowards without any thought for the people they are leaving behind. They have no understanding of the impact their actions will have on their nearest and dearest, who are left to clear up the mess and deal with the guilt for the rest of their lives.

Wrong. That's not correct. Those are not the right conclusions.

The vast majority of people who attempt to commit suicide are mentally very unwell. The chemical imbalance affecting your brain makes it impossible for you to think rationally because your mind is broken. It is not functioning properly. The neurotransmitters aren't doing their job.

When you break your leg, you can't walk; when you are horribly depressed, you can't think.

In fact, it's worse than that. You can think, but you can't think straight. Your thinking is completely distorted and twisted. The extreme depression is playing evil tricks on you, lying to you. It's telling you that you are a burden on all those around you, that you're dragging them down, that the world would be an infinitely better place without you.

By the time you attempt to take your own life, you have already departed from this world. You have done so because you believe you are doing the right thing, the selfless thing, the brave thing. Your damaged mind is telling you this every minute of every hour of every day. Eventually, you believe it, because it becomes too painful not to.

That's precisely how I felt.

Christine Skoutelas, blogger and freelance writer, sums things up colourfully and accurately:

'Depression lies. It's a horrible asshole bitch that breaks people – it breaks good people, strong people, loving people, grateful people. It does not discriminate. It's an equal opportunity fucker.'[26]

Final point. I would like to apologise to the lorry driver for any distress this incident may have caused you. I hope this narrative makes it crystal clear that it was completely my fault, not yours.

CHAPTER 9

SALVATION

The Trauma Service Unit at the John Radcliffe Hospital in Oxford provides treatment for patients who have sustained life-threatening physical injuries as a result of major accidents. A 24-hour service is provided by a dedicated team of consultants and specialists, including both neurosurgeons and plastic surgeons for reconstructive surgery after serious injuries. I needed the former but fortunately not the latter.

I would remain a patient there for two weeks.

The Beauty of Simplicity

The first thing I remember when I regained consciousness was talking to Mel and one of her closest friends who had accompanied her to the hospital. The second thing I remember was making a somewhat lewd joke and all of us laughing out loud. The third thing I recall was getting mildly frustrated with the head nurse who I felt was not being either sympathetic or patient enough.

It is difficult to explain just how significant those relatively insignificant moments were in the immediate aftermath of my accident.

Conversing, laughing, complaining. On the face of it, nothing special, nothing worth writing home about. But they represented three small signs of life, three "normal" everyday behaviours I had not displayed in months. Not only was I utterly relieved to be physically alive, a miracle in itself, but more importantly, I was relieved to be alive emotionally again. I had been in the darkest of tunnels for several months, but it felt like I was now finally emerging into the sunlight.

However, I remained incapacitated and bed-bound during my first week in hospital. My lung was being drained, my head wounds were healing slowly, and I was still in a lot of pain. From time to time, I would also burst out crying for no particular reason. I was very fragile and still had a whole bunch of horrible memories festering away in the back of my head, just itching to re-surface. Initially, the doctors took me off all the medication I had been on before the accident. Mel intuitively sensed something about me was different. She encouraged them not to put me back on the cocktail of drugs but to see how things progressed. They listened to her and agreed with her non-expert's diagnosis.

It was the second week of my stay I remember with greatest clarity because it signalled a gradual return to a wonderfully boring normality. What did this look like?

I was now able to walk and would pass the time of day cruising the sterile hospital corridors, attached to my drip, smiling inanely and chatting happily with the other patients and nurses about everything and nothing. I would buy the newspaper and turn straight to the sports pages just like the good old days. I would treat myself to a Mars bar at 11 every morning in the hospital cafeteria and savour every bite. I would go for a gentle stroll in the Japanese garden every afternoon, soak up the sunshine, smell the flowers, and suck in the fresh air. I would get visits from my family and friends at teatime and talk about nothing more serious than the day's news and the weather. I would sleep soundly for 10 hours every night without the fear of waking up.

It was ground-breaking progress.

In the words of Sir Winston Churchill, 'Out of intense complexities, intense simplicities emerge.'[27]

I now had a "proper" physical illness, one I could almost be proud of, and one which made a lot more sense to everybody around me. It was much simpler to explain away a bicycle accident and a collapsed lung to fellow patients than it was to talk about the impact of stress at work and the symptoms of agitated depression. In fact, colliding head-on with a truck made for quite a colourful corridor conversation, but obviously I decided to miss out the suicide bit.

No doubt about it, my two-week stay in hospital marked a turning point. Being knocked off my bike was the pivotal moment. I will never really understand what flicked the switch back on. Was it the physical impact caused by the accident to my brain? Some kind of high-risk shock therapy? Was it the awful realisation that I had come within a whisker of losing my life, my wife, and my kids which had finally brought me to my senses? Or was it something else? Something more divine?

The 2010 Copiapó mining accident in northern Chile began on Thursday 5th August with a cave-in at the San José copper–gold mine. Thirty-three men trapped 700 metres underground and five kilometres from the mine's entrance spent 69 days living in darkness. They survived in dangerous and claustrophobic conditions. A five-inch wide hole became the miners' lifeline, a vessel for food, water, and supplies, and this alone kept them both sane and alive until all 33 were finally rescued on 13th October. Among the miners, a number attributed enormous religious significance to their eventual rescue. One of them, Mario Sepúlveda, said, 'I was with God, and with the Devil – and God took me.'[28]

My mother-in-law always firmly believed it was the hand of God that had given me a second chance.

The Slow Road to Repair

It was now the beginning of August, time to recuperate and start the slow process of recovery, both mental and physical. Having spent a fortnight in hospital, I was finally given permission to return home. Mel would spend a further two weeks driving me to Oxford on a daily two-hour round trip to receive intravenous drip antibiotics. These were treating a bacterial infection called empyema I had picked up in hospital.

My two business partners had kept in touch with Mel during this period and Andy had paid me a visit when I was in hospital. They had both been understandably shocked to hear about my accident and were oblivious to the fact that it had been a suicide attempt. It was not something I owned up to at that time. To anybody. In fact, it was a little secret of mine that would remain hidden for many years to come.

Meanwhile, a detailed letter outlining the process for my departure from Brand Learning and the purchase of my shareholding had arrived in the post. This confirmed the details of my telephone conversation with Andy a few weeks earlier when I was so desperately ill.

Neither Mel nor I were ready yet to deal with such matters. In just under four months, I had not opened my computer once or looked at anything vaguely work-related. My body and mind were still very tender, still healing. So, this letter was put to one side for the time being.

To this very day, it remains a mystery why this period didn't signal a return to the living nightmare. After all, nothing was significantly different. My situation at home had not really changed. I had simply been given a brief respite, a fortnight off from the crushing solitude, the utter desperation. I had no job to go back to and no financial security going forwards.

But the strange thing was that life wasn't the same as it had been before the accident.

Those feelings of utter misery, total desolation, and complete isolation had now left me. I had been purged. Cleansed. Admittedly, I experienced a few wobbles after my departure from hospital, some tears, and a sudden panic attack or two. The memories of the last few months and the surreal drama of the previous few weeks were still very fresh in my mind. We remained understandably worried about what the future might have in store. Nevertheless, things had slowly started to feel different. The fog had lifted slightly, I was beginning to think and act like a normal human being again. Or a newly born foal taking its first tentative steps into a strange, new world, not completely steady on its feet, but getting there, bit by bit.

After finally being signed off by the hospital, the family decided to go to Bournemouth on the south coast for a few days. A truly memorable holiday. Just being able to join my kids making sandcastles, enjoying a Cornetto ice cream, feeling the warm sun on my face, taking mid-afternoon naps. Precious little luxuries. A month or so earlier, I had been marooned in the Mariana Trench at the bottom of the Pacific Ocean. Now I felt liberated standing on top of Mount Everest on a clear and sunny day.

Life is a funny thing.

When I was writing this section of the book in July 2018, I was intrigued to know whether any of my kids had any recollection of the summer of 2001. Will would have been seven years old, Emily five, and Jack two. I remembered the extreme guilt I felt at the time when I was no longer communicating with them in any meaningful kind of way. I asked Will on the assumption that if anybody remembered anything at all, it was going to be him. His memories were vague and distant, nothing concrete. He seemed to recall a couple of visits to the hospital and a lot of serious-sounding adult conversations, but nothing more.

I was relieved.

Before moving on to the next chapter, I feel the strong desire to say something important.

If you are thinking about it, don't do it. Don't throw yourself in front of a truck, don't jump off a tall building, don't take an overdose. Even though you might have found yourself trapped in the darkest of caves, there will be a ladder somewhere, an escape route to the surface. That ladder might be a combination of time, talking therapies, medication, and the love of those around you, but it will be there. You must believe that. And best of all, when you find it and climb to the top, the light will be brilliant and sparkling. Life will feel more intensely wonderful than it ever was before.

So, just don't do it. Trust me.

CHAPTER 10

DECISIONS, DECISIONS, DECISIONS

The honeymoon. That special time when everything is picture-perfect. You've just enjoyed the best day of your life, marrying the one you love, surrounded by your family and closest friends. You get some ring-fenced time to reminisce about the great day itself, indulge yourself wherever you happen to be, and look forward to the excitement of your journey ahead. A protected period for you to be spoilt and pampered without any feelings of guilt.

Everything new goes through a honeymoon phase of sorts, whether it's the arrival of a baby, the first few weeks in a job, or the joyful experience of picking up your brand-new car. My convalescence during the first three weeks of August was my equivalent and the feeling was no less exciting.

In my case, what was new was life itself.

Mel and I continued to feel a sense of complete and utter relief. Firstly, I was alive, physically and emotionally. Secondly, I much preferred waking up to being asleep. And thirdly, we were back to enjoying all the little things in life. Walking the dog, going to the pub, mowing the lawn, having sex again.

I had now been prescribed the slow release version of Efexor XL (75mg) which I was to take for the next six months. This was intended to keep my mood steady and stable. I was still assigned to my psychiatric nurse, and his job was to keep a watchful eye on me and make sure I didn't inspect any more railway lines too closely. We would meet every couple of weeks to review progress and check how I was doing.

During late August, I began tiptoeing my way back into the workplace. I entered my home office, the scene of my previous suffering, to discover my work computer was no longer the man-eating lion it had been four months previously. It was a huge relief to be able to turn it on, process what I was seeing in front of me and start working methodically through my very short to-do list.

My brain was allowing me to function once again. The mental engine had re-started five months after it had conked out. The breakdown was officially over.

Time to Decide

Mel and I now needed to make some important decisions about our next steps.

I had resigned over the phone to Andy at the height of my illness, just over a week before my "accident". It was clear to me that going back to Brand Learning in my previous role was not going to be in my best interests from a mental health perspective. I would not have been able to fulfil my obligations as a director at that time. Everything was still so very raw. It would have been like a fireman walking back into a burning house, stark naked and without a hose. Complete madness. I still had third degree burns.

I reconfirmed my resignation.

Now it was just a question of agreeing the terms of my departure from the company, and Mel and I had to confront the financial and legal documents that had been waiting patiently for our attention. The numbers and mumbo jumbo were back for one final time. To be honest, neither of us had much appetite to dive into the details. In any case, all the paperwork we had received seemed to be in order and well documented.

My two partners had offered to cover the costs of getting advice on the Compromise Agreement from a solicitor. I had been sent this to check over and sign. This is a specific kind of

contract between an employer and an employee where the latter usually receives a negotiated financial sum for resigning as an employee. The benefit to the employer is they are able to draw a line under an employee's departure and are protected from any future claims. The Compromise Agreement is linked to matters of employment only.

This is quite different to a Shareholders' Agreement, a binding contract between the shareholders, that covers areas such as the sale or transfer of shares and the process for resolving disputes. Before my illness, I had led the development of this document, and with input from professional advisers, the three of us had all discussed and agreed the numerous clauses contained within it. I was now leaving the business and one of those clauses clearly stipulated I was obliged to sell my 33% shareholding back to my two remaining partners.

However, Mel and I believed my contribution to the birth of Brand Learning and the role I played in the initial set-up of the company should be recognised. What's more, my exit from the company was taking place in quite exceptional circumstances that none of us could have reasonably predicted. I wasn't a "bad leaver", departing under any kind of black cloud, or setting up in direct competition. I was a "good leaver" and would indeed remain loyal, working with the company for many years to come.

So we asked Andy and Mhairi if we could retain a small shareholding. We felt this was the least my efforts deserved, irrespective of what was written in the Shareholders' Agreement. But we were turned down.

This was very disappointing, but I didn't ask a second time. The truth of the matter is I was still experiencing a huge sense of guilt, having cost them four months' sick pay, as well as all the stress and grief during that period. I also felt fortunate that the door to a possible return to Brand Learning as an independent consultant remained open. Business was booming, the company would soon be moving into new offices on the River Thames, and I didn't want to jeopardise an opportunity that could lead to regular income. We were very nervous about the future, and we had neither the courage nor the conviction to rock the boat.

Our chief concern remained the state of my mental health, and the number one priority was not to place it under any more undue pressure.

So I met Andy and Mhairi on the 26th August to go through the documents and I also reviewed the numbers with the company's accountants. On 6th September 2001, I signed away my share of the company.

It was a very poignant moment. The dream had just died.

But at least I was alive and kicking rather than pushing up the daisies. It was time to move on. The party was finally over. The last few months had been a sad and unfortunate chapter in my relationship with the company I had co-founded. However, the 12 months I had spent helping set up Brand Learning had undoubtedly been, in equal measures, by far the most exhilarating and stressful period of my business career.

Two Painful Lessons

Daniel Handler is an American writer and musician, best known for his children's series *A Series of Unfortunate Events* published under the pseudonym Lemony Snicket. He coined an insightful quotation around the vagaries of fate:[29]

'Fate is like a strange, unpopular restaurant, filled with odd waiters who bring you things you never asked for and don't always like.'

Before moving on with my story, I need to fast forward to an event that took place many years into the future. It will demonstrate how a fateful discovery helped unearth two salutary lessons about the perils of making life- or career-defining decisions when you are mentally unwell.

I was up in our attic at home looking for a business book when I stumbled across a folder with the words "Brand Learning 2000 / 2001" written on it. It contained all the legal and financial documents relating to the time of my illness which I had kept. I was just a little intrigued, so I decided to take the folder downstairs to have a look at the contents.

Once I had finishing skimming through the paperwork, my curiosity only increased. I felt slightly troubled by what I had read and a little nagging voice in my head was telling me to get a second opinion from an expert. One of the mistakes I felt I had made back in the day was not seeking the right advice from the right people.

One thing led to another and before long I was meeting up with Antony Morris, a highly professional lawyer and an equally compassionate human being.

The first question he posed was why I had resigned over the phone back in July 2001 when I was mentally so unwell. I told him I felt very guilty that my continued absence was putting my two partners as well as the start-up under increasing pressure. I also hoped this decision might serve to alleviate the levels of extreme stress I was then feeling.

Antony's strong advice at the time would have been not to have taken this course of action. In his view, I should have waited until I had fully recovered before deciding anything of such significance.

He then proceeded to quiz me about a number of things, including the Shareholders' Agreement, the critical document in the folder. He asked me whether I was aware it had remained unsigned when I sold my shareholding back to my two partners. I replied that I was aware of this. Although it wasn't signed, I had led the final document's development and we had all agreed the clauses within it in principle. Therefore, I assumed it was legally binding.

Antony told me that, for the very reason it was unsigned, it was possible that the Shareholders' Agreement might not have been legally binding. Therefore, it was conceivable in retrospect that I might **not** have been under any legal obligation to sell my shares to my two partners when I did, the September after my accident. There was no hurry. I could have hung on to my shares until I had fully recovered or maybe negotiated a better deal than the one I had got from the net assets valuation method we had used.

What was difficult to digest when Antony dealt the hammer blow was that back in August 2001, Mel and I had specifically asked my two partners if we could retain a small shareholding. We felt this was well deserved. Although I had bailed out of the rocket prematurely, I had played a key role in getting it into space. But Andy and Mhairi stuck firmly to the terms of our Shareholders' Agreement. The request was refused at the time and this had really hurt.

Antony also pointed out that clause 3.4 in the same document had expressly given my two partners the power and discretion to allow me to keep some or all of my shares when I left the company.

This made things doubly disappointing.

I must confess I did feel somewhat of a retrospective idiot. If there could be such a term. Let's be honest, you would think it would have been the obvious thing to do to check out the Shareholders' Agreement, the most important of all the documents, with an independent lawyer. Especially when you knew it had remained unsigned. That was an elementary mistake, wasn't it? A pretty big one too.

Other than disappointment, there was one other emotion I felt very strongly. Anger.

We Learn

But as they say in life, you win some and you lose some. There was nothing Mel or I could do. The Limitation Act meant we were time barred from making any claims even if there were any to be made.

And to be fair all round, we were a start-up business with everything happening at a million miles an hour. My illness had put a lot of pressure on everybody. It wasn't easy for anyone. I realise that. As a result, mistakes were probably made all round and I for one could certainly now see the errors I made back then.

In 2001, mental health in the corporate arena was not the hot topic it is now. It was misunderstood by the majority. During the last few years, most organisations have finally begun to take it very seriously. And it's about time they did. The second National Employee Mental Wellbeing Survey, carried out in 2017, highlighted the worrying fact that 60% of the workforce experience mental health problems because of work.[30] However, what remains equally disturbing is that only 53% of all employees feel comfortable talking about issues like depression and anxiety.

The first figure is far too high, the second far too low.

When we discovered the documents in the attic, the waiters had certainly brought Mel and I things we hadn't ordered, and they turned out to be ones we didn't particularly like. But the silver lining was that this episode did help me draw out two important lessons about mental health, both of which are very relevant in the current climate.

Firstly, *avoid making any kind of major decision when you are mentally ill*. I discovered that stress and depression can do all sorts of strange things to your hippocampus, prefrontal cortex and amygdala, none of which are very conducive to rational thinking. There's a time for big decisions but it's not when you are at the bottom of a deep and dark pit. The consequence of making ill-informed choices could end up being life-changing. So, don't make them.

Secondly, *if you do need to make important decisions during a period of mental illness, put all your trust in the independent experts who know what they are doing*. Let them hold your hand and do all the complicated thinking for you. They will have the technical knowledge you don't possess and won't be emotionally attached to the matter at hand. This is certainly not the time for any do-it-yourself decision-making. Get yourself an Antony. They will be worth every penny.

Back to the Present

For better or for worse, Mel and I were blissfully ignorant of all of this in the early autumn of 2001. We would remain so for many years to come.

Back then, I was just grateful to be alive.

Although I was eager to start the rebuilding process, I must admit I was also slightly nervous as to what lay ahead. Was my Big Blip really over or was it just in some kind of cruel remission, waiting to re-surface when the moment was right? I was also unemployed with financial obligations. How could I be sure that freelance work would be available for me, even though it had been promised? And if there was work on the table, would I be up for it? Would I still have what it took to perform in front of a class full of challenging participants?

A lot of uncertainty was hanging in the air as 2002 approached.

CHAPTER 11

THE 10-YEAR WORK / LIFE BUSINESS PLAN

Decompression sickness (DCS), also known as divers' disease or the bends, most commonly refers to problems that arise from underwater diving decompression. In other words, it's what happens whenever a diver returns to the surface too quickly. The gases dissolved in the body turn into bubbles on depressurisation and bubbles aren't good news. DCS can produce many symptoms including joint pain in the shoulders, elbows, knees, and ankles. In some severe cases, it can also lead to paralysis and even death.

The recommended ascent rate is about 10 metres (33 ft) per minute, and a decompression schedule, involving a number of planned stops, must be carried out as necessary. This requires the diver to ascend to a particular depth and remain there until sufficient gas has been eliminated from the body to allow further ascent.[31]

Best practice for a person re-entering the workplace, having suffered a period of mental ill health, should follow exactly the same procedure. In both cases, you should emerge from the deep and dark place you have been to, slowly and safely, supported by those around you. Pushing the diving analogy further still, what you ideally need is a "dive buddy", a companion who "has your back", and who looks out for you as you begin to ascend from the murky depths.

When somebody has suffered a full-blown mental breakdown, "returning to the surface" too quickly is particularly dangerous if the environment at the surface was the primary cause of the breakdown. The re-entry needs to be managed carefully and sensitively.

Antonio Horta-Osorio, CEO of Lloyds Banking Group, returned to work "70 per cent" restored after his well-publicised breakdown back in 2011, following a nine-day stint in the Priory Clinic in London. At the request of the Board, he began seeing a psychiatrist immediately after his return to work and this ongoing treatment lasted several months. He continued taking sleeping pills, weaning himself off them gradually. He undertook dietary changes and was in bed by half past ten every night. Back at work, he also allowed himself two or three "spare" hours every day to undertake the daily grind of the job, like answering emails and writing presentations. His stock began to soar again as Chief Executive and it soon became business as usual, albeit with some very important safety measures now firmly in place.[32]

This is a good example of a well-managed rise to the surface with appropriate decompression stops and support built in at each stage of the recovery process. It enabled Horta-Osorio to return to the top of his game, equipped with a much greater level of self-awareness.

My First Decompression Stop

My "accident" had taken place on the 19th July 2001. I had spent two weeks recovering in hospital before taking the next couple of months off to get back into decent mental and physical shape.

It was now October and I felt strong enough to start resurfacing. My ascent from the depths started off pretty well. Although I was no longer employed by Brand Learning, I was able to continue my relationship with them as an independent consultant and this presented me with my first "decompression stop". I came back into the fold as a management trainer, running courses for clients I had worked with before my illness as well as new ones the company had acquired since.

This was a win-win situation for both sides. I badly needed the income and Brand Learning needed my expertise on both the training and learning fronts.

Before I had become ill, I could perform this kind of work in my sleep, and it was a huge relief to realise I hadn't lost my abilities in the classroom. It was one thing discovering you could turn on the computer without freezing but quite another to find out you weren't going to clam up in front of 30 demanding Unilever graduates, all keen as mustard, hungry for your attention, and thirsty for new knowledge.

Although the analogy might seem uncomfortably close to the bone, that first decompression stop was like getting back on a bicycle after a nasty fall and being relieved to find out that you still had the confidence to ride again.

The real bonus was having my passion for what I had previously loved return in spades. My enthusiasm for work was almost child-like. It was as if the four-month horror show which had taken place earlier in the year had acted like some kind of surrogate sabbatical. My broken mind had been given the opportunity not only to recover fully but also to reboot and reinvigorate itself. It was positively raring to go.

This gave me renewed energy for the job. Long-haul business class to far-off destinations like Tokyo and New York were joyous events again, little oases of pleasure, rather than the monotonous drags they had become during the last couple of years. The strain of corporate jobs to be done had given way to the joy of in-flight movies, power naps, and plenty of peanuts. Running five-day workshops was no longer the tedious slog of old but an opportunity to let my creative juices flow once more and experiment with new techniques in the classroom. I was loving it. The cat had once again got the cream. The petrol tank was now full, and the engine was running more smoothly than ever before.

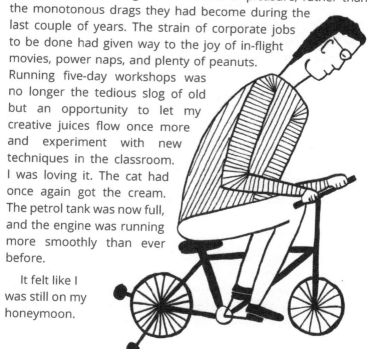

It felt like I was still on my honeymoon.

Wonder Woman Mel

During the period of my illness, Mel had been a superhero, the rock that had held everything together – the family, the house, and, as far as it was possible, me. She even managed to find the energy to hold herself together throughout the crisis. Since my "accident", she had experienced conflicting emotions.

On the one hand, there was the unbridled joy and relief that she had got her husband back in all senses of the word. After all, she had been just a tyre's width away from becoming a widow and facing the prospect of having to bring up three young children on her own. She now relished the simple and normal things in life again. No more hiding knives, or talking to psychiatrists, or visiting suicidal husbands in trauma units. On the other hand, she still endured feelings of doubt and uncertainty. Was my upbeat mood going to last or would it be a false dawn? Was something ugly lurking around the next corner? For her, the enormous contrast between life before and after the accident was still hard to comprehend.

During the time I had known her, Mel had never been seriously ill, but just before Christmas in the year of the Big Blip, an irritating cough turned to bronchitis which in turn became pneumonia. She had to spend three days in hospital so that doctors could keep a watchful eye on her and manage the infection. She had held out all this time but now she could finally give in to the demands of her body and mind. She had given herself permission to take some over-due "me-time" to recover not just from the illness but also from her *annus horribilis*.

Mel would never admit it, but I am sure she was just a little relieved to be given the chance to have some time away from me, the kids, and the house. A mini-break of sorts. The doctors probably felt it was a good idea too. Having said that, 72 hours in a mixed ward, surrounded by old men snoring and farting, while suffering from a nasty bout of pneumonia wouldn't have felt much like the long weekend in Paris she richly deserved.

The small consolation for her was the knowledge that I was now in charge of sorting out the drudgery of the daily to-do list at home in Stewkley.

After Mel's few days in hospital, we were finally able to draw a thick line under 2001. We very much hoped 2002 would turn out to be less eventful and much more dull than the previous year had been. From that point on, we continued to enjoy all aspects of our lives as a family and there were no signs of either my anxiety, stress, or depression making an unwanted return.

Phew!

But that's not to say 2001 was entirely bad. There was one small surprising, but welcome, silver lining that emerged from that year. Mel and I started talking to each other properly again. During much of my thirties, with me striving to get ahead on the work front and Mel spending most of her time wrapped up in the children, weekday dinners became functional experiences. Food was consumed quickly to fuel up before I returned to my emails and Mel continued with her household chores. Even worse, we would often switch on the small TV in the kitchen for half an hour while eating. Talking was replaced by mindless viewing. This changed during the intense period of my illness when the television remained switched off during dinner, and conversation, although heavy and depressing in nature, returned between the two of us.

Once the depression had lifted, Mel and I made a conscious decision we would always eat together, never have the TV on again at dinner time, and talk to one another about all things, both major and minor. It doesn't sound very ground-breaking, and as I write this, I do feel slightly embarrassed even mentioning it. After all, isn't that just what "normal" couples do? But it was very important for both of us to draw lessons from what had happened. Our marriage had certainly never been in trouble or on the rocks, but we had been in danger of becoming disconnected from one another, following different trajectories, drifting further apart. It was not so much a question of rebuilding our relationship but more one of re-igniting it.

The Second Decompression Stop that Never Was

A lot of my freelance work was now being carried out through Brand Learning.

Although the company was growing rapidly, it was still relatively small at the time, a boutique agency in both look and feel, employing only a dozen people or so. Given my background, I remained the authority on training, the "go to" person, and the newcomers who joined the organisation would often turn to me for guidance and support. They were experts in marketing, many arriving from senior roles in major companies, but most were relatively inexperienced in the art and science of capability development.

Working alongside Sam Ellis, one of the company's first full-time joiners back in 2001, I helped codify best practice in the art of workshop design, development, and delivery. What I relished about this role was helping others acquire the same skills I had developed during the last 10 years. Everyone around me seemed so hungry to learn and I was only too willing to impart my knowledge. Although I was just freelancing and no longer a part of the core management team, I still felt I was an important cog in the company's wheel. I also had a strong appetite to learn about the subtleties and intricacies of marketing from all my new colleagues who were much more experienced marketers than I had ever been. It was a symbiotic relationship.

This supportive and inclusive environment helped me flourish once again, and, as a result, I became mentally stronger and stronger.

However, as I look back on this period, I do have one nagging regret I have never quite been able to put to rest, one question that remains unanswered in my mind. I wonder whether I should have made a bigger effort to move up to the next "decompression stop" more quickly and take on some management responsibility within my area of expertise. The danger about not making the next step is you can get too comfortable with where you are and lose the belief that you have what it takes to make the next jump. Your mental muscles adapt to your resting point and become more and more reluctant to flex and grow. You run the risk of staying put and stagnating. Stagnation then leads to boredom which in turn can lead to frustration, and before you know it, that increasing sense of frustration can take you back into tricky waters again.

Some species of shark, including the great white, must swim constantly to keep oxygen-rich water flowing over their gills.[33] If they stop moving, they die. It's the same for a career: it's important to keep moving in some direction, any direction. Otherwise, you run the risk of dying professionally through a lack of stimulation.

A learning director or something similar was what I had envisaged at the beginning of the Brand Learning journey, a position where I could have developed my thinking and led the capability agenda. I would have been much more qualified to do this rather than dip into the worlds of finance and the law, where I struggled. I wrestled with this option internally and broached the subject with Andy, now my ex-business partner, but it seemed the door for re-entry was closed shut. There wasn't too much appetite to have me back as a permanent employee at this point. To be brutally honest, I don't blame either of my two ex-partners for their reluctance to consider this seriously. Why would they take another chance and risk what had happened before? In any case, the company was going from strength to strength and my absence from the top table was hardly being missed.

But even as I write this now, 16 years on, I am not quite sure whether that particular "decompression stop" would have been the right one to take. I couldn't fully trust my own motivations. Why did I really want "back in"? Was I still grieving the lost opportunity of running my own company, something I had come so tantalisingly close to but had now slipped through my fingers? Clinging on to the dream that was slowly drifting away? The fifth Beatle looking enviously over his shoulder, witnessing the meteoric rise of the other four? Was I still living in denial that the Big Blip had really happened and had I already carelessly forgotten the enormous pain it had caused me and everybody around me?

Or was it just my Winner gene whispering desperately in my ear, 'Go on, son, just one more go'? After all, I now felt on top of the world once again, capable of doing anything. But maybe that was the danger. Despite everything that had happened to me in 2001, I might still have been tempted to take the wrong path. What I came to realise at the end of 2002 was I now needed to take the rebuilding programme seriously if I was going to stay clear of any potential pitfalls.

The rebuilding programme would consist of four phases, taking place over a three-year period.

Phase 1 – Coming Out of the "Mental Health Closet"

The first important phase surrounded my attitude towards the breakdown. Mental illness was a pretty taboo subject at that time, not something that was talked about either by people who had suffered or by those who were suffering. However, I was very open about what had happened to me. I didn't really have much choice. It had been a very public affair. I had helped to start a fledgling business, with two high-profile partners, which was going extremely well. I had bailed out early, taking four months' sick leave before having a major road accident and then returning to the world of employment as a freelancer. This would have been tricky to conceal from clients and colleagues. 'I just had a bad virus that took a frustratingly long time to clear up …' would not have fooled anyone.

The other reason I came clean was I didn't really think I had anything embarrassing to hide. I had nothing to be ashamed of. I felt I had more to gain by being completely transparent and that others had more to gain by my honesty. During one of the first workshops I ran back in the US a few months after my return to work, I remember spilling the beans about my story to a small group of young graduates at the end of the day's training. Rather than being uncomfortable with what I was sharing, they remained captivated and curious when I explained, warts and all, what had happened, why it had happened, and the lessons I had learnt about myself.

At that time, I missed out the "suicide bit". I think it might have freaked them out and I still wasn't ready to be quite that honest.

The third reason I felt comfortable talking about my Big Blip was because it was extremely cathartic, even though this catharsis was often accompanied by a tear or two. Things were still quite raw.

Phase 2 – Working with Sue

What I discovered over the next 18 months is having a sounding board to help you navigate your way through the recovery process can be invaluable. As you move from one decompression stop to the next, you need somebody to hold a mirror up, ask the hard questions, provide support, and challenge your assumptions if necessary.

In 2002, my first full year back in the workplace, I had become more and more bullish about things, and my ambition was beginning to inch its ugly head above the parapet. There was a danger that Winner gene would start to dominate Worry gene once again. My golden rule about staying sane was getting the balance right between the two genes, satisfying both their needs. But sometimes, I forgot the rule. Or simply ignored it.

I had to make sure my next decompression stop was the right one. Mel had done a wonderful job of supporting me through my illness and we would continue to have many a conversation around what to do next and what not to do. But although she was now only too aware of my strengths and many weaknesses, her lack of detachment and objectivity persuaded me to look for somebody "on the outside" to help me see the wood from the trees. I needed an experienced professional to hold my hand through the next phase of my journey.

What I needed was a "dive buddy".

Dr Sue Holland was that person. She had significant experience working in the corporate sector for Unilever as their Global Head of Coaching but was now pursuing the life of independence as a coach. Her approach involved working in the present in a person-centred way, and its goal was to facilitate transformational change within the individual. It required high doses of intuition, understanding, and human empathy. It also demanded exceptional levels of skill in listening, questioning, and appreciating.

Sue possessed these attributes in abundance. She simply got it and she got me. Our first meeting took place at the very beginning of 2003. Many years later, I asked Sue what her first impressions of me were during that session.

She had this to say:

'You showed immense openness, but this was accompanied by a sense of lostness. You seemed "de-shackled" from corporate life and, as a result, you were vague about what the future held. You still seemed very vulnerable, and I felt you were a little bit like gossamer, a very fine material that needed to be handled with extreme care.'

Underneath my bullish surface, I was still quite delicate, and memories of that time remained painful. Sometimes, it felt like it had all happened two days rather than two years ago. Sue was not a therapist and so she had to demonstrate due diligence of care. At the beginning of every session, she would always ask me where I was mentally and emotionally on a scale of 1 to 10. 1 equalled "top of the world", and 10 "bottom of the pit, suicidal".

Fortunately, I had remained a long way off 10 for some time now.

After a couple of sessions, we started to explore what I wanted as far as my career was concerned. We drafted a desired outcome ('I will be financially successful working from a place that maximises who I am') and then Sue helped me explore why I wanted this, what I visualised over the next five years, and what the next steps might look like. She would always ask the right questions to help me explore potential avenues, but always left it to me to decide which path to take.

She used different methods from her toolkit depending on what I brought to our conversations. On one occasion, she left me with a book to read between our sessions – *Jonathan Livingston Seagull* by Jonathan Bach, a quirky novella about a seagull learning about life and flight. The main message centred on the importance of self-discovery.

'You have the freedom to be yourself, your true self, here and now, and nothing can stand in your way.' ... 'The gull sees farthest who sees highest' ... 'What he had once hoped for the flock, he now gained for himself alone. He learned to fly and was not sorry for the price he had paid.'

The book helped me understand I was free to choose a different route in life, one that might end up being less conventional, less corporate, and less constrained by structures and systems. I understood perfectly that my Winner gene needed nourishing, but I was beginning to better understand how to nourish it in the right way.

A mentally safe way.

By working closely with Sue, I came to the conclusion that a full-blown return to corporate life as an employee would not have been the right option for me. I wanted to make progress, to advance my career, but I realised I needed greater freedom if I was going to reach my full potential as an individual in the business world.

This seagull needed to fly a little.

So, very gently and skilfully, Sue helped me stay focused on the path of independence I had chosen; a path where I could flourish in so many other ways. She wanted me to take the next step but more than anything, she wanted me to make sure it was the right one. It didn't have to be vertical. I didn't have to climb higher and higher up the corporate ladder. There were other directions I could take.

My Worry gene liked Sue. She had a straightforward way of helping me make difficult decisions. She was a great "dive buddy".

Phase 3 – Learning by Observing Others

The third part of my rebuilding programme was to look around me for inspiration, studying others who by their actions and attitudes could guide me in the right direction. Two people who influenced me significantly during the rebuilding process were my two ex-partners.

As an outsider looking in, it was a fascinating exercise to observe both Andy and Mhairi leading the company. Mhairi was completely in her element, driving the business forward with incredible stamina and an insatiable appetite for work. She seemed to have the ability to lap up and absorb any problems that arose, both minor and major. She was very commercial, strategic, and focused on her goals and took enormous pleasure and pride in taking a small start-up all the way to a thriving international consultancy. She was also determined to pioneer a flexible way of working at Brand Learning. For example, she was very committed to helping women fulfil their ambitions both as working professionals and as mothers.

Andy, who is extremely smart and approachable, found it easy to forge strong relationships with both colleagues and clients alike. He also possessed the ability to grasp the big and the little picture at the same time. It was very clear just how proud he was of founding his own company. And rightly so. In the later years, as the business became bigger, more complex, and as it started to change direction, Andy was astute and self-aware enough to find a different environment, a new passion in the area of leadership where he could play to his considerable strengths.

What both of them taught me, especially in the early years of Brand Learning, was that there is a direct correlation between sustainable mental health and job satisfaction. I admired the way in which they drove the company onwards and upwards, year after year. But this success only came about because they enjoyed what they were doing and they were also extremely competent at it. They didn't seem to struggle with the burden of their responsibilities and always looked very comfortable in their own skins.

Mhairi liked running the business. Andy enjoyed driving excellence in marketing. They had found and followed their passions and their personalities provided the perfect match.

What they also both did very well was recruit the right kind of talent into the company. Not just individuals who were compatible with the strong culture they were keen to develop, but also people who had the personalities and make-up to help the company grow and grow quickly. Many of the new joiners had cut their teeth in big organisations like Unilever, Proctor and Gamble, Mars, Pepsico, Reckitt Benckiser, and PwC. They had all gained significant experience managing resource, people, and budgets, and, as a result, they seemed very comfortable doing the same kind of thing, albeit in a smaller environment.

Every employee and freelance consultant felt very much at home within the Brand Learning set-up and it showed. They were living proof that the secret to career contentment really wasn't rocket science. You put yourself in the right conditions, surround yourself with the right people, do the right kind of work, and you will probably flourish. If you don't, then you may well flounder, and floundering is often the start of the slippery slope of mental decline.

Brand Learning would go on to achieve a top five place in the *Sunday Times* 100 Best Small Companies to Work For listing from 2009 to 2012. By the time the company had been bought by Accenture in 2017, the workforce had grown to over 170 people, led by an accomplished team of directors and shareholders. They had offices in three continents and had even managed to persuade Niall FitzGerald, former chairman at Unilever, to join the company as its chairman.

It's not possible to pull this off in a job you don't enjoy.

However, here's the rub. I would often reassure myself that what Andy, Mhairi, and many other very capable people at Brand Learning were doing was not right for me. We were just cut from a different cloth. Their heaven was my hell and probably vice versa. Many of them enjoyed managing resource and taking big decisions. I didn't. But I felt completely at ease in front of 30 challenging participants running a three-day workshop in Shanghai, where English was most definitely not the first language in the room. Many of them didn't.

By the end of 2003, two and a half years after my breakdown, I had taken a number of steps to rebuild my broken mind. I was slowly beginning to get a much better sense of what I was all about. In the words of Sade Andria Zabala, the poet, 'I understood myself only after I destroyed myself. And only in the process of fixing myself, did I really know who I was.'[34]

Whenever I left the Brand Learning offices in Hampton Wick after one of my frequent visits, there was always a smile on my face as I made my independent way home around the busy M25 motorway.

Phase 4 – Developing My "Business Plan"

A quick recap of the rebuilding process so far:

Phase 1 was "coming out of the 'mental health' closet" and being open, honest, and transparent about my Big Blip. Phase 2 was the coaching I received from Sue, my dive buddy, over a period of 18 months. Phase 3 was developing a much better sense of who I was and who I wasn't by learning from others around me.

Phase 4 would bring all of this together.

I have always loved the theory of everything. I take pleasure in playing with business models and frameworks, taking them apart, rebuilding them, creating hybrids, trying things out. I was a tinkerer. Like a kid with a pile of Lego bricks. Two by two and three by three matrices, graphs, Gantt charts, spider diagrams, pyramids, and circles. I could never get enough of them. And it wasn't just in my professional life I was addicted to theory; it ran through into my personal life too. For example, I kept a little notebook that captured the tips from all the golfing and skiing lessons I had ever received.

Do. Reflect. Plan. Practise. Do again. This was the traditional learning cycle that should underpin any well-constructed training course. My notebook represented the Reflect and Plan stages. In my view, this discipline was best practice if you wanted things to stick and if you were serious about making progress with anything in life.

Mel and the children were always very dismissive about my conscientious approach towards self-improvement. They took great pleasure in mocking both me and my little book. And even though neither my golf nor my skiing have made much progress over the years, a lack of natural ability rather than learning methodology is probably to blame.

I realised there were tools and techniques I had used on my training courses in a corporate setting which, with a little bit of tweaking, could be adapted for use on a personal level. One of these was a relatively well-known model used to help brands and businesses plan for both the short- and the long-term. This could really assist the rebuilding effort.

Fundamentally, a business plan is made up of three different elements all of which build on one another:

1. Where are you at, and what are your strengths and weaknesses?

2. Where are you heading both in the long- and short term?

3. How will you get there?

Pretty basic stuff.

So, one day, I hid myself away and had a go at drafting a "business plan" for myself. I couldn't afford to get things wrong again, so my natural inclination was to find a disciplined and structured way of getting things right this time around. What I produced was a watered-down version of a genuine business plan, but it worked for me and it certainly helped feed my theorist's appetite.

So here it is, step by step:

Where was I at?

My Performance Review was an honest assessment of how things had panned out since 2000, when we set up Brand Learning. My self-analysis was a mixture of both personal and professional factors because I wanted the exercise to be a holistic one. If I were going to live a different life, then I would need to *plan* for a different life. A lot of the material forming the basis of the "business plan" had originated from the coaching sessions I enjoyed with Sue during 2003 when she had encouraged me to tell the whole truth.

When it came to pinpointing my strengths and weaknesses, it was important to be as honest with myself as possible, particularly as far as the latter were concerned. Fortunately for me, there was plenty of hard and incontrovertible evidence from the recent past to call upon. Mel was only too keen to contribute here as well.

1. Performance Review	
Work	**Home**
• I hadn't enjoyed my short stint as an entrepreneur • I had lost and then regained my love for management training • I enjoyed travelling abroad again, but not excessively so	• I was enjoying spending more time with friends and family • I had regained my sense of fun and humour after it had been lost in the wilderness for a year or two • In a nutshell, my life was now becoming more balanced

2. Strengths and Weaknesses	
Strengths	**Weaknesses**
• I was good at communicating • I was empathetic and supportive of others around me • I had a decent sense of humour • I was a very good trainer • I was creative (as yet untapped) • I was self-supporting and independent as an individual	• I was prone to stress and anxiety under pressure • I was not very decisive in the presence of others • I was not very good at managing resource or people • I was sometimes unrealistic with my goals and ambitions

Where was I heading?

I wanted to develop a long-term vision of the future that wasn't narrowly focused around work alone. This had been my biggest mistake during my thirties when an obsessive desire to move on and up the corporate ladder, at the expense of savouring life in the moment, had not done me any favours. Ironically, I would later come to realise that the better balanced your life, the more productive and successful you were likely to be in the workplace.

I was now tiptoeing in the right direction.

3. Long-term vision
• To work hard and play hard
• To enjoy a full-on lifestyle as a family
• To lead a rich and varied life, full of mini-adventures

How would I get there?

The word "strategy" is much over-used and abused in the world of business. 'A plan of action designed to achieve a long-term or overall aim', is one dictionary definition.[35] Unfortunately, the term is often thrown into conversations by insecure executives when attempting to elevate their own status among their peers.

My strategies were important, but I wanted them to be very short term, things I could execute tomorrow, not in six months' time. They were more like tactics, concrete and tangible actions that could make an immediate impact on my life. I also wanted to put plans in place that would start to deepen the relationships I had with both my friends and family. The key thing was to ensure these were realistic and achievable.

No laughing now, please.

4. Strategies and tactics	
Strengths	**Weaknesses**

Mark department
- Make time for exercise three times a week
- Work five days a week from 8am until 6.30pm latest; five weeks holiday per year
- Keep close to Brand Learning as a freelance consultant
- Stop trying to climb the corporate ladder
- Grow horizontally, learn, and develop myself in the world of marketing learning
- Put together an ambitious and realistic annual work plan, to include financial targets, areas for professional development, number of fee-earning days, number of days spent away from home

Mel dept.	**Will, Emily and Jack dept.**
• Keep the TV switched off at dinner time • Discuss both little and big things • Spend more time together • Hold hands more often	• Pick up the kids from school • Tell Jack a bedtime story whenever I can • Watch Will and Emily playing sports matches, performing in plays, etc. whenever possible • Always be present for my kids, mentally and physically

Social life dept.
- Think about and care more for others around me
- Focus on friends you want to have for life (and not just for Christmas!)
- Look for depth rather than breadth in friendship
- Look out for people suffering from mental ill health, be open about my experiences and encourage them to believe it's going to be okay

I suspect a large percentage of readers will be chuckling quietly now at this slightly sad attempt to bring the world of business into the personal arena. At face value, it does seem a little bit over the top, I must admit. But this was how I was, how I still am today. It's my way of getting through life. I've always loved theory more than practice, and I am sure this is one reason why I have always gravitated towards education. As the saying goes, 'Those who can, do ... those who can't, teach.'

However, I also bet there are quite a few closet "theory nuts" right now, nodding approvingly. You know who you are.

In Sue's coaching sessions, one of the metaphors she used that always resonated with me was around "banisters and rickety staircases". She wanted to help me create a strong set of personal banisters that would keep me steady and stable. A support network, good habits and routines, a positive mindset, and medication if required. Life would always have its ups and downs, it would always be somewhat of a rickety staircase. But the banisters should always remain firm and secure. The business planning approach was part of the woodwork.

I knew where I was heading in theory. It was now time to put that theory into practice.

CHAPTER 12

GOING FOR GOLD

It was now 2004 and time to execute the plan. Although I knew success was ultimately dependent on my being able to achieve that elusive work / life balance, I always felt, in my case at least, if I got the work bit right, the life bit was likely to follow suit.

According to popular wisdom, there are two types of career growth – vertical and horizontal. The former is climbing the corporate ladder in a straight line and taking on additional managerial responsibilities along the way. This path requires you to master other people. This hadn't worked out for me at Unilever where the pre-ordained journey from trainee to marketing director in 10 years hadn't materialised. I hadn't got past the second rung.

Horizontal career growth, on the other hand, is migrating across the organisation, giving you the chance to work in new functions, encounter a cross-section of contrasting personalities, and providing you with the opportunity to expand your thought leadership in separate areas of the business. This path doesn't necessarily require you to master other people, but it does enable you to master yourself. I hadn't exactly covered myself in glory when I got a sour taste of the finance and legal professions at Brand Learning back in 2000 / 2001.

I would now take a different but equally rewarding career path. I didn't want to go up the ladder. I didn't want to go across it. I wanted to climb down it as far as possible. I had spent the last 10 years at MTP and Brand Learning skimming the surface of marketing, my chosen area of expertise as a trainer. I had become a competent all-rounder and knew a little something about most topics including strategy, planning, communication, consumer understanding, and innovation. But now I wanted to excel at just one thing, and that one thing was consumer understanding. More specifically, consumer insight. This discipline was the "new kid on the block" in the corporate arena and any big company worth its salt was embracing it. It was the foundation of everything within marketing. If you understood what motivated consumers, what

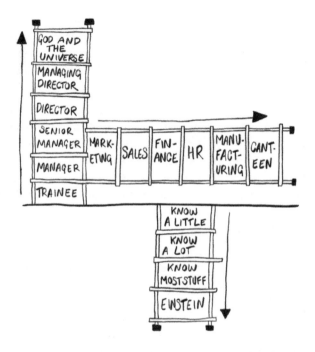

made them tick, then you had a better chance of developing new product ideas and services that uniquely met their needs. You could communicate with them more effectively, because you would know how and where to reach them and which messages to convey.

For the next seven or eight years, I launched myself head first into the subject. I read up on everything, I hunted for best practice, I ran workshops for organisations across all sectors in all parts of the world. I developed proprietary thinking in the area, trademarked a term that I subsequently sold for a substantial sum of money. I had articles published in leading business magazines, gained a strong reputation around this topic within my professional sphere of influence, and took enormous pleasure in helping others excel at the difficult practice of insight generation.

My Winner gene was being given something to be proud about, but equally importantly, my Worry gene was being kept happy at the same time. By both focusing and stretching myself within my comfort zone, there was less danger of things unravelling again. In fact, the longer my pursuit for mastery in this area continued, the safer and more secure I became mentally. The self-confidence and certainty that came with deepening knowledge and expertise acted as a mental safety blanket. Constantly pushing myself to learn new things also meant I wasn't getting frustrated, and so the reservoir in my brain was continually being topped up with fresh stimulus.

In short, I took great delight in what I was doing. You don't hear of many breakdowns in the workplace because somebody enjoys their work too much. 'Find out what you like doing best and get someone to pay you for doing it.' The words of Katharine Whitehorn, the British journalist, hit the nail on the head.[36]

My Portfolio Career

I was 42 years old now and for the next 13 years, I would experience a range of different working environments, bumping into a whole bunch of alternative, creative, and wonderful professionals.

I continued to work as a freelance consultant with Brand Learning, and this remained my major source of income for years to come. I was very fortunate to be working with a company still going from strength to strength.

They valued the contribution I was making towards the business, particularly in my specialist areas of learning and insight development. The approach I had pioneered around the latter was now widely used by the company's broad spectrum of clients across the globe. I also learnt bucket loads from the many expert professionals around me, having lots of fun along the way.

It was always a Win:Win relationship.

During this period, Mhairi asked me if I wanted to re-join the company as a learning director, a position I felt would have been best suited to my talents when Brand Learning was still in its infancy. But now, it had become a "proper, grown-up" company. The management team had put solid systems and structures in place, essential components if the business was to continue its upward trajectory.

However, I was now addicted to the freedom of picking and choosing my projects, working only to the usual deadlines these projects demanded. I could decide how much work I wanted to commit myself to, and this luxury of being able to carefully manage my workload helped keep the pressure levels low. I was enjoying the liberated feeling of not being accountable to anybody and of setting my own priorities. I still treasured a strong sense of "team" by working closely with others on client projects, but I didn't need to be employed by the company to provide me with any further sense of belonging.

I remained an introvert at heart and still loved being a seagull.

I was very flattered by Mhairi's offer but I declined. At this point in time, the financial security I was enjoying operating as a regular freelance consultant for the company, as well as the benefits I was getting from its excellent infrastructure, allowed my creative juices to continue flowing, stress free. I was good at what I did, and I remained in demand as a result. I was determined to stick to the plan because it was working.

There was no need to change.

At the same time, I carried out a significant amount of interesting work for another excellent capability agency called Imparta. When working with them, I remained the primary source of intellectual property on the projects I signed up for, because their focus was on building sales rather than marketing capability. This meant I was given even more autonomy and control than I had at Brand Learning, but the trade-off was that I enjoyed less intellectual input and inspiration from those around me. Working with both organisations, the balance between structure, support, financial security on the one hand, and both autonomy and control on the other helped maintain and strengthen my mental stability.

I had the best of both worlds.

In addition to working with corporate giants like Unilever, Shell, Barclays, Nokia, British Telecom, and Lloyds, I also collaborated closely with a whole smorgasbord of smaller organisations and one-man bands on all sorts of quirky little projects, often for love rather than money.

I offered advice to Trish Munro, a village friend who was setting up an exciting business venture called the Yoga Factory, an offering for schools that provided children with the physical and mental benefits of yoga. I provided some consultancy to Chris Green who had walked away from a conventional career to create an online business called Charlie Vegas. This supplied promotional mascot costumes throughout the UK to people and organisations. I helped two dynamic entrepreneurs who ran a great little company called Golden Acre Dairy Foods identify opportunities for one of their brands in the protein shakes market. I carried out one-to-one coaching with the Head of Press and Marketing for Cameron Mackintosh, producer of *Les Misérables* and *Phantom of the Opera*. And some years later, I would commit to delivering an annual lecture on creativity to more than a hundred sixth-formers at my younger son's secondary school in Hertfordshire.

One week I might be running a three-day workshop in the US for 25 young eager beaver Unilever graduates. The next week, I could be on a train to Manchester discussing how to sell more fancy-dress costumes online during the busy Christmas period ... with a conversation on how to market yoga into schools taking place sometime in between.

My mind was always buzzing with new ideas, looking for ways to learn from all the projects I was working on. Cross-fertilising and making random connections are the very essence of creativity. Albert Einstein called this combinatory play.[37] You are grappling with a tricky problem, a tough nut to crack. You try all the usual avenues, but they yield little. You walk away from it and engage in a completely different activity, ideally one you enjoy. But you leave your mind wide open to play with the lingering problem. Thoughts connect and collide in your sub-conscious before you finally get rewarded with that magical "AHA!" moment.

In the case of Einstein, he would use a violin break as his form of escape. Whenever he was stuck on a problem, he would put it to one side and play the violin for a few hours. During that period of relaxation, combinatory play would take place in his brain, and more often than not, he would suddenly get an idea for how to solve the problem he had left behind.

Just like that.

This variety of all the projects, both big and small, meant I continued to nurture and nourish the creative part of my brain. It was continually restocked with stimulus rather than strained with boring stuff that would drain away the juices.

And remaining in total control of both my workload and my destiny meant that my stress levels remained well clear of the red zone.

Creative Creatures

A further source of stimulation was born in 2008, when I started working with a dynamic Danish maverick called Hanne Kristiansen. The free-spirited Hanne personified creativity itself, always questioning, challenging, and brimming full of what might be possible. I was now 46 and Hanne was a few years younger. She lived and worked in Barcelona, having recently swapped the world of Kellogg's for the freedom of life as an independent. Based on a unique approach in creativity, conceived a few years earlier by Hanne and a colleague called Pippa Hodge, Hanne and I set up a company called Creative Creatures.

I was very conscious to learn from my Brand Learning experiences, so we did things differently:

Firstly, neither of us put all our eggs in the one basket, both retaining a sense of independence and continuing with our own consultancy businesses at the same time. Financially, this would have been too risky in any case, with the new venture initially generating next to no income. It would only have got my Worry gene twitching nervously again.

Secondly, we were both aligned on the kind of "company" we wanted to develop. We had both left organisations to avoid the need for systems, structures, and schedules. So, we kept things loose, agile and fluid, communicated once a week via Skype and that was usually enough.

And thirdly, although we differed as individuals in many ways and had the odd disagreement now and then, we respected each other both personally and professionally. Our differences were compatible and made us stronger together. We had developed something proprietary and unique, we were earning money from it, and were enjoying the ride.

Avoiding the Enemies of Creativity

Within this brave new world of independence and unburdened by the shackles of corporate life, I was now setting my own agenda. I found this liberating. I worked on projects with other free spirits and our "offices" might be the British Library in London, a Costa coffee shop in Oxford or a motorway service station on the M1. I treasured the sense of freedom. I didn't miss time sheets, budgets and forecasts, office politics, or the scramble for car park spaces. My inbox, although busy, rarely overflowed, my phone never rang incessantly, and the most frequent text messages I received were from Mel.

The more independent I became, the more I did my best to avoid the enemies of creativity. Deadlines were one of the chief culprits. I craved time and space to mull things over, play around with half-baked thoughts and fledgling ideas. I needed to be able

to toss them around for a bit in the mental melting pot. This was the very essence of my creative process, but it demanded the luxury of inefficiency. I tried hard to shy away from fast-moving environments, where decisions had to be taken yesterday. I needed tomorrow and the day after. Douglas Adams, the English author, really nailed it when he said, 'I love deadlines. I love the whooshing sound they make as they fly by.'[38]

The Golden Summer

It had been a golden decade which came to a glorious climax in 2012.

For any sporting aficionados, this was an awesome year to be British. Chelsea became the first London club to win the European Champions League; Bradley Wiggins the first British rider to triumph in the Tour de France; Europe enjoyed an astonishing comeback to snatch victory from the Americans in golf's Ryder Cup; Andy Murray captured his first tennis Major at the US Open; England mauled the usually invincible All Blacks at rugby. And we haven't even started talking about Jessica Ennis, Mo Farah, and Nicola Adams at the Olympics, or Ellie Simmonds, David Weir, and Hanna Cockcroft at the Paralympics. It was a feast to gorge yourself on and I kept on consuming sport all year long.

As a family, we also had a good summer. Will was now 18 and would be heading off to Manchester University after his gap year; Jack was 13 and would succeed in getting through to his secondary school of choice; and Emily found herself at the top of the podium with an outstanding set of GCSE results that enabled her to move into the sixth form with flying colours.

When I reviewed the "business plan" developed back in 2003, I found myself ticking many of the boxes. I had successfully executed several of the strategies and tactics I had intended to put in place.

Mark. My life was more balanced now. I had managed to stick with the right career ladder and had boosted my professional reputation within my chosen area of focus. I continued to work closely with Brand Learning and had a good relationship with both Andy and Mhairi. And even though I had to keep my eye on income levels week by week, month by month, they had remained sufficiently high for us to enjoy a comfortable standard of living. I also kept myself in pretty good shape physically. And although walking the dog energetically and playing golf badly were probably not the equivalent of exercising hard for 45 minutes, three times a week, I wasn't too far off the mark. *8 out of 10.*

Mel. The kitchen TV remained switched off during dinner. We talked more as a result (and not just at dinner time) and made sure we did more things together as a couple. She continued to manage the household but also took on a part-time job as a learning support assistant at a local school. There was still room for improvement in the "hand-holding" department. *7 out of 10.*

Will, Emily, and Jack. One of the things I was most pleased with during this decade was that I spent much more time with my children than I would have done without the blessing of the Big Blip. The path of independence had made this possible. I watched them playing in their school matches, performing in plays, singing in musical concerts, not just at weekends but whenever I could during the week. And when I wasn't abroad on business, I was always much more "present" with them at home than I had been for much of my thirties. I managed to avoid the tag of Distant and Detached Dad. *9 out of 10.*

Social Life. This flourished. Mel and I began to deepen our existing friendships and, although we negotiated hard at weekends to satisfy our conflicting introvert and extrovert requirements, the negotiations remained generally peaceful. However, I would always remain open and available to those around me who had found themselves in difficult mental places. I had acquired a heightened awareness of friends and colleagues, particularly those in the business arena who seemed jumpy, distracted, or solemn looking. Individuals who were usually quick to respond with emails but had suddenly gone missing in action were always on my radar. I was now more skilled at identifying the early warning signs of mental ill health in others and I was never frightened to probe and ask the question, 'Are you alright?' *9 out of 10.*

33 out of 40. Room for improvement in all categories, but yes, overall it had been a very solid effort.

As I looked back on the period between 2003 and 2012, it had been, on balance, a very satisfying decade. So good that I would give it an impressive 8.5 out of 10.

And although we were slightly disappointed with the bronze medal (at least Winner gene was), I understood the reasons why we had missed out on either gold or silver. The decade that had just finished had given us only one very sad event to deal with on the personal front. The death of my mother-in-law, Lorna, who died from cancer aged 75. On the work front, my chosen career as an independent had not placed us under any amount of financial pressure. So it would be fair to say that the banisters had not really been fully tested because the staircase of life had remained fairly solid.

To have any chance of winning gold, you would need to pass a much sterner test than the one I had just undergone.

I had suffered a major breakdown in 2001 and all the evidence suggested I was now repaired. I was confident those repairs would be perfectly adequate if I wanted to cruise down the motorway in fifth gear for the rest of my life. But would they be strong enough to complete the Dakar Rally, travelling 9,000 miles across Peru, Bolivia, and Argentina? How would I fare going off-road, encountering difficult mountain terrain with rocks, sand dunes, mud, and all kinds of other obstacles and challenges?

I was now going to find out whether the repairs were adequate or not because everything would change in the autumn of 2012. Our lives would get turned upside down and we would spend the next five years in the trenches, dealing with matters of life and death.

All my experiences as a mental health sufferer would now be required in a new role.

This time as a father and carer for my daughter, Emily.

PART II

CHAPTER 13

THE ANOREXIA WARS KICK OFF

(October 2012 to April 2013)

WAITING FOR ANA

On 5th May 2012, our daughter, Emily, turned 16. She was just a regular teenager going through the ups and downs of adolescence. She was kind and considerate towards others. Level-headed, sensible, and talented in many walks of life, including drama, dance, and netball. She was very sociable and loved to party but was also very hard-working on the academic front. She would go on to achieve an excellent set of GCSE results that summer.

In September of that year, she entered the sixth form at Aylesbury High School to begin her A Levels. A month or so later, Mel came in to my study at home with a slightly worried look and said, 'We need to talk about Em.'

She had been making herself sick. One of her friends had become suspicious of her behaviour, had shared this with her own mother, and they had both confronted Emily. They encouraged her to speak to Mel and said if she didn't, they would feel they had no choice but to tell her themselves. They were both very worried about Emily and were only acting in her best interests.

Our daughter came home and confessed. She had developed an eating disorder.

Our initial reaction was low-key. From the outside, nothing seemed to be drastically wrong. Emily might have lost a couple of pounds or so, but it wasn't significant enough to really notice. Besides, she was doing a lot of exercise at school, was heavily involved in a dance show and a musical theatre production as well as playing netball two or three times a week. We had put the weight loss down to a busy schedule. And even though we acted immediately by making an appointment via our GP with the local Child and Adolescent Mental Health Services (CAMHS), in the back of my mind, I viewed this as something that would get fixed soon enough. Mel and I were aware of both anorexia and bulimia, but we were not fully informed about either the causes or the symptoms. We didn't know anybody within our circle of friends whose children had suffered from either illness. This ignorance meant we weren't at panic stations quite yet. Give it two or three months, I felt, and she would be as right as rain, full steam ahead, little blip over. I remember Mel being less certain.

Six years later, when we sat with Emily at a restaurant on the island of Mallorca and saw her eating a plate full of food like any other young adult, I looked at her and told her how proud I was she was finally eating normally again.

Six long years.

The Enemy, Anorexia Nervosa

Anorexia nervosa, usually referred to as anorexia, is an eating disorder, characterised by an aversion to food and drink. This results in low weight and a fear of gaining weight and this food restriction is often driven by a strong desire to be thin.

In the late 19th century, anorexia became accepted as a bona fide medical condition when Sir William Gull, one of Queen Victoria's personal physicians published a paper where the term "anorexia nervosa" was coined.[39] It was only during the latter half of the 20th century, in 1978, when the German-American psychoanalyst Hilde Bruch published *The Golden Cage: The Enigma of Anorexia Nervosa* that the science of the illness came to the attention of society at large.[40]

The exact causes of anorexia are unclear, but research and evidence suggest it is probably a combination of biological, psychological, and environmental factors.

Although it is unknown which specific genes are biologically responsible for the illness, it appears that individuals with a genetic tendency towards perfectionism and the need for control have a greater likelihood of developing anorexia.[41] Psychologically, people who have obsessive-compulsive traits find it easier to starve themselves of food whether they are hungry or not. The drive for perfectionism causes them to believe they are never quite thin enough, even though the outside world may hold the polar opposite view. There is no doubt that the rising importance of body image in society, in particular among the young, and the accompanying peer pressure driven by social media, have only served to fuel the flames.

The facts are disturbing: in data published by Beat (the UK's eating disorder charity) and MIND (the mental health charity), 1.6 million people in the UK struggle with an eating disorder; 14–25-year olds are the biggest group; 1 in 100 women suffer from anorexia; and 89% of total sufferers are female.[42] Most disturbing of all, a review of nearly 50 years of research (Arcelus, Mitchel, Wales & Nelson, 2011) confirms that due to the effects of weight loss and starvation on the brain, anorexia nervosa has the highest mortality rate of any psychiatric disorder.[43]

During the next few years, Mel and I were going to discover what a brutal, relentless, and unforgiving enemy we were up against. We would come to realise that its single-minded objective is to kill its victim and it is prepared to go to any lengths, however underhand, to achieve this goal.

Dropping, Dropping, Dropping

When we were first referred to the CAMHS unit in November 2012, Emily's weight was around 50kg or 110 pounds, giving her a Body Mass Index (BMI) of 19.5. The minimum healthy BMI for someone of her age is 18.5, the maximum 24. When fully fit and healthy, Emily's weight had been 54kg (119 pounds), giving her a BMI of 21. So it was nothing serious yet, but dropping nonetheless. We were concerned that Emily was restricting her food, skipping lunches, and still making herself sick. She was at school all week with complete responsibility for her own intake.

The weight continued to drop.

By December, it had fallen to 48kg (106 pounds), a BMI of 18.7, hovering close to the 18.5 mark. Christmas lunch wasn't much fun that year in the Simmonds household. During the first couple of months of 2013, she struggled through school, finding it more and more difficult to keep up with the workload requirements.

More worryingly, the anorexia was beginning to take up a disproportionate amount of the thinking time and mind space she had available. This was placing an ever-increasing strain on her levels of concentration. She seemed to be doing everything possible to avoid eating and the resulting weight loss was leading to a rapid decline in mood. Her brain was beginning to buckle and she was becoming clinically depressed.

Midway through the spring term, we took the collective decision, along with her teachers, CAMHS, and her GP, to pull her out of school and try to manage her illness full-time at home. The AS level exams were now only a few months off and Emily couldn't cope with the pressure anymore. Preserving her health trumped the need for making academic progress.

The weight still continued to drop.

By the end of February 2013, Mel had become a full-time carer for Emily at home with the support of the CAMHS team. I was still working flat-out to keep the money coming in, so my role was part-time. Between us all, we would supervise meals six times a day, seven days a week. The problem at school was it had been too tempting, too easy to miss meals. At home, we would endeavour to ensure nothing was ever missed and that she consumed every last morsel of food on her plate. Every mealtime, either Mel or I would sit alongside Emily and encourage her to do the one thing she didn't want to do: eat.

But the weight continued to drop pound by pound, and we were now becoming more and more perplexed and confused. And very worried.

We soon began to understand what we were up against. We were fighting an enemy who knew every trick in the book. Mel and I were two amateurs playing against a seasoned professional. Ana (the ironic term of affection we gave the illness) possessed a variety of weapons in her armoury. They were used at different times but always with the same outcome in mind: weight loss.

Here is a selection from her impressive arsenal:

Concealment. Even though we would be sitting right next to or directly opposite Emily at mealtimes, Ana would teach her how to conceal her food when our gazes were diverted for a split second. Emily would slip a biscuit stealthily down her bra or hide it in her socks. After the meal, she would either flush the evidence down the toilet or conceal it in various nooks and crannies around the house. We would make some grizzly discoveries over the next few years.

Purging. After the meal had finished, Ana would encourage Emily to visit the toilet, stick her fingers down her throat, and regurgitate the remnants of the food she hadn't hidden. A few grams of "excess weight" would then disappear down the drain.

Water-loading. Ana would remind Emily to drink lots of water the night before her weekly weigh-in to provide a false picture of her weight. This would give everybody the misleading impression that she was eating well and gaining weight. Very clever.

Laxatives. Ana would urge Emily to buy laxatives from the local chemist to ensure her bowels remained empty, free of any food and drink ... and calories. Sneaky one. It took us a while to work that one out.

Exercise. All of a sudden, Ana and Emily started going on long and purposeful walks around the village to get some fresh countryside air ... and burn off a few more unwanted calories in the process. If we ever tried to ban her from doing so, all hell would break loose. Either that, or she would agree not to go out, lock herself away in her room, and carry out an intensive session of sit-ups and push-ups.

Point blank refusal. And if Mel and I ever managed to supervise meal times so strictly that Emily and Ana couldn't pull the concealment trick out of the bag, then they would reveal their trump card. They'd look at the food placed down in front of them with disdain, refuse to eat, and walk out of the kitchen.

No negotiation. That simply wasn't fair. A bit like a child playing a game and when it becomes too difficult or they start losing, they just give up.

ANA'S ARMY

And that's why the weight continued to drop. It was now 41kg (90 pounds), with a BMI of 16.

It had been a bruising six months for all of us, and each member of the family dealt with Emily's illness in different ways.

Mel – Joint Commander in Chief

It just wasn't right. First, she had to put up with me back in 2000 and 2001. Alice, my mother, then came to live in our village in 2004 in need of our love, care, and support. She had found life on her own on the south coast increasingly difficult since my father had passed away. She remained ravaged by both anxiety and depression and required constant, daily supervision. And nine years later, Emily completed the set. Mental illness in the Simmonds family had spread across three consecutive generations. Mel would have been well within her rights to look towards the heavens and scream very loudly, 'Why me? What have I done to deserve this? It's just not fair. Please God, just give me a break!'

Mel didn't say any of that, and knowing her, she probably didn't even think it. That just wasn't her style.

But it was heartbreaking for me to witness how the mother / daughter relationship began to buckle under the strain. Whereas Emily's peers were now all turning 17, going on shopping trips with their mums to buy new clothes, and sharing their first glasses of Sauvignon Blanc together, Em was camouflaging her emaciated body in baggy clothing, drinking calorie-free Diet Coke, and hiding biscuits inside her pockets.

Mel's way of dealing with the anorexia was to provide Emily with rational, logical, eminently sensible solutions. 'If you don't start regaining weight, you are likely to develop osteoporosis', 'If you don't get your periods back soon, this will significantly reduce your chances of having kids', 'Just think what those poor children in Ghana would say if they saw you now' (referring to her World Challenge trip of the previous year). Emily never reacted positively to that kind of advice because her mind was damaged and distorted. It just wasn't on the same wavelength as Mel's.

As a consequence, the lack of communication and understanding between mother and daughter often ended in ugly shouting matches, verbal fisticuffs, and prolonged sulks on both sides. On many occasions, I had to play the role of a neutral referee, pulling apart two boxers who had resorted to fighting dirty, sending them back to their respective corners to regroup and calm down.

Being piggy in the middle wasn't easy.

Mark – Joint Commander in Chief

Once I realised we were in it for the long haul with Emily, I resigned myself to the fact I would have to live with depression on the doorstep. I was surrounded by the "old enemy" once again.

The golden decade suddenly seemed very long ago.

Whenever I found myself in the company of Emily, I appreciated what Mel must have experienced 12 years previously: dead eyes, distant looks, pale skin, lethargy, feelings of hopelessness, pessimism, despair, unpredictable mood swings ... I could go on. Being under the same roof with somebody like this for days, weeks, and months on end is draining and debilitating. But I understood all this. I mean I really, really understood this because I had been to the place where Emily was now. I felt the pain my daughter was going through very acutely and I suffered alongside her.

But here's the thing.

Across the entirety of Emily's illness, there was only one time I crumbled. And that crumbling only lasted a few hours. It was early on in the Anorexia Wars and after that episode, I became more mentally resilient. Overall, I held firm, and I am very proud of that. My own defences shored up and Sue's banisters remained in place. Of course, like Mel, I was deeply concerned, desperately sad to see the life being sucked out of our daughter. But there was no collapse, no deserting the sinking ship. To be honest, I didn't really have a choice. There wasn't any room left in the house for any more mental health disorder. We had Ana and she was more than a handful, taking up far too much space as it was. Now was not the time for me to be weak when what was at stake was the life of our daughter. And the longer the illness progressed, the stronger my resolve became.

Fortunately, I could also tap into my previous experiences of mental ill health. My approach to dealing with Emily was fundamentally different to Mel's because I benefited from having been on my daughter's side of the fence. Intuitively, I knew which tactics were likely to resonate best and which ones wouldn't. Although, like Mel, I would occasionally feel the need to hammer home the serious implications of not eating, I would also try to appeal to Emily's irrational and emotional mindset.

I would sit down with her on her bed, hold her hand, ask her how she was feeling, listen carefully to what she said, empathise, and remain non-judgemental. I would reassure her the "real Emily" was just taking a short holiday, that she was in hibernation, but when she emerged, she would be a new and improved version. I told her to look into my eyes and I asked her to trust me. I promised her she would be alright. At best, I knew those words would only give her a glimmer of hope and a sliver of comfort, but that was better than nothing.

Hugging helped too. Both of us.

I needed to find ways of keeping myself on the mental straight and narrow. My professional work proved to be a welcome distraction, a temporary escape from Ana, but the only type of work I felt comfortable with was the basic "bread and butter" stuff. Work I could do relatively easily, on automatic pilot, without thinking too hard. I just didn't have the mental bandwidth to compartmentalise things, and Emily's illness always seemed to seep into everything else I did. Anything requiring too much creative thinking or imagination was out of bounds. My brain wasn't up for any of Einstein's combinatory play.

Our beloved pet project, Creative Creatures, was put on the back burner for a couple of years. In fact, it took an extended holiday for another very happy reason. My partner, Hanne, became a late mum giving birth to a beautiful daughter, Sunna. Hanne made the very conscious decision at that point to throw all her energies into motherhood for the time being.

So Creative Creatures entered a period of dormancy.

Fortunately, a large proportion of my training and consultancy work in 2013 was UK-based, so I was never too far away from the battle on the home front. That was the good news. The bad news was that Ana would often follow me into the training room like a bad smell. There were many occasions when I was standing in front of a class and a message would silently flash up on the screen of my mobile phone. An angry- or desperate-sounding text or voicemail would be waiting for my attention. Mel was tearing her hair out at home and needed either moral support or practical advice.

There were times I wished I could have returned to the good old days, when I could only get in touch with Mel by going outside and making a call from a telephone box. This would have allowed me to deal with the illness on my own terms. Unfortunately, anorexia, just like any mental illness, operated according to its own timetable. It would never strike any deals with us.

It was only ever a ping away.

The other way in which I tried to cope with the situation was to fall back on my introverted nature, shut myself off in my study at home, and resort to the one thing that always helped me make sense of things. Theory. I was able to repurpose some of the approaches I used in my profession as a management trainer to help Emily fight Ana. I made it my mission to try to understand the illness as best I could. I read books, researched articles online, and spoke to people who had recovered from eating disorders. I produced weight charts, plotting the history of her decline and forecasting how long it would take our daughter to get back to a healthy BMI if she started eating properly.

I produced all kinds of checklists for my own consumption but would only ever share with Emily material I felt might inspire or incentivise her. My daughter was a very visual and kinaesthetic person in terms of how she learnt and absorbed information. She was not going to pick up a 300-page self-help book on "how to beat anorexia in 90 days" and apply the lessons the next day. That wasn't her style. She responded to Post-it notes, colour, images, pictures, and inspirational quotations. So I encouraged her to develop mood boards to illustrate what life could look like when she recovered, to list all the fabulous places in the world she would visit one day, to identify the exciting jobs in years to come that would be right up her street. I figured that if the future could be made to look bright, this might incentivise her to escape from the prison of the present.

Sometimes it felt as if she was a participant on one of my workshops. To be fair, Emily was a far more attentive student than many of the ones I did have. Perhaps that's because there was more at stake.

The Troops

In 2013, our eldest son, Will, was in his gap year and would start his degree at Manchester University during the autumn. He was at home for the first half of that year, when Emily was ill. For two and a half months over the summer, he went travelling with a couple of school friends to the Far East. He'd be fortunate enough to miss most of the carnage during the next few years. Of course, he did his best to support us whenever he was back home, but it was difficult for him to know what to say or do. We were finding the whole thing tricky enough to understand ourselves, so we could hardly expect a young adult to be any wiser or more insightful. It was also somewhat of a relief for Mel and me having one less person in the house, one less person to worry about.

However, Jack, who was only 13 when it all kicked off, was less fortunate. He found himself caught up right in the middle of the mayhem. He had to endure the sight of watching his older sister deteriorate in front of his very eyes, which was particularly sad as he had enjoyed a close relationship with Emily over the years. They had developed a tightly knit bond which was become looser with every passing day. God knows what he made of it all.

We suspect Jack internalised things a lot and tried to work things out in his own head. A small silver lining of Emily's illness was that Jack learnt how to become self-sufficient and independent. He didn't have much choice. He also had the good fortune of going to an excellent school where the teachers kept a watchful eye on him, and he had a whole gang of mates who kept him distracted from the troubles at home. Jack was mature enough to grasp he could only ever be the centre of attention for very short periods and he  understood the focus of his parents needed to be elsewhere. He was never greedy for our time.

As far as our black Labrador, Purdey, was concerned, she provided everybody with the love and loyalty only dogs can offer. In the most difficult of times, she gave us some welcome and uncomplicated relief. However, one thing that did slightly confuse us for a while was she started putting on weight. Funny, because it coincided with the time Emily started losing weight. At least somebody in the house was benefiting from our daughter's illness.

My Little Blip

By the time we got to the end of March, it's probably fair to say Ana had claimed her first two victims: Mark and Mel. We weren't knocked out yet, but we were fighting a losing battle. We were on the ropes. We were no longer in control of the situation and we had simply run out of ideas. We needed reinforcements.

At the same time, my mother's health was deteriorating. She was 81 years old and had recently experienced a number of bad falls in the house. She was becoming incontinent and required even closer supervision. I continued to pay her daily visits and started looking for a care home nearby. She was no longer able to look after herself safely and she had trouble getting herself up and down the stairs. Mel shared the load. She had become the daughter Alice never had, and they both now enjoyed a very strong relationship. They had become particularly close after the death of Mel's own mother a few years before.

Eight months later, Alice would die from lung cancer.

And to complete our trilogy of challenges, just before Easter and a week before he was due to leave for five months of gap year travelling, Will experienced a serious injury playing rugby. He was now convalescing at home where he would remain for the next couple of months until the injury healed enough for him to travel. This wasn't life-threatening by any stretch of the imagination, but it just felt like one more thing on top of a whole host of "one more things".

All those years ago, Sue had told me the staircase was bound to become rickety from time to time but that the banisters, if well looked after, would always remain firm. I think that my staircase was now on the verge of collapsing completely. And without a staircase, banisters have no obvious purpose.

I was hanging on for grim death.

I tried my absolute hardest to practise all the things I had preached to myself since 2001. I took daily exercise, either cycling with friends or walking Purdey. I managed my workload so that it remained sensible and achievable. But coping with everything happening around me was becoming increasingly difficult. The Chinese water torture effect was back with a vengeance. A drip here, a drip there.

I had been here before. I remembered.

So, on Friday 5th April, I decided to visit the doctor. I explained I was feeling under pressure and maybe it was a sound idea if I went on medication as a precaution. A pre-emptive strike of sorts. My doctor agreed and prescribed a small dose of citalopram to keep the depression at bay and zopiclone to help me sleep at night. I hadn't been on this kind of stuff since the Big Blip. The doctor also contacted one of the psychiatrists at the Tindal Centre, the Adult Mental Health Services Unit in Aylesbury, informing him of my condition and asking for an urgent assessment. He was aware of my history and he knew where this might all end up. I guess he was taking precautions too.

For the next few days I soldiered on, but I was becoming more and more agitated. I couldn't concentrate on anything for very long. I became increasingly detached from the rest of the family and locked into my own thinking. There was too much going on in my head. Twelve years previously, it had been all the stresses and strains associated with setting up a new business. Now it was Alice, Will, and the burden of finding a solution for my deteriorating daughter. My brain was filling up with problems I wasn't able to resolve, and I couldn't turn off the tap. I couldn't even find the tap.

The pressure was mounting.

The Man-Eating Lion Returns

Drip, drip, drip.

It was Tuesday 9th April. School holidays.

Mel was out, dropping Jack off with a friend, and keeping Emily occupied at the same time. Will was in the house, his full arm in plaster, not complaining, accepting his bad luck, just getting on with life, like he always did.

I entered the home office and started the day's work.

I turned on the computer and looked at my to-do list. I began with the first item but couldn't make any progress. Déjà vu. My head was brimming with Alice, Emily, and Will. There was no mind space left for work. But I had to work. I was once again the sole bread winner in the household, and even though I would have welcomed another extended holiday, a four-month "sabbatical" to sort out the big issues, I didn't have that luxury. Back to the to-do list. *Come on, Mark, just get on with it*. Nothing was going in. My disk was full. I left my office and went into the kitchen for a coffee. Another déjà vu. Mind starting to race. Back in my office 15 minutes later. To-do list. Nothing happening. Frozen. Bugger.

Drip, drip, drip, drip.

I stood up and started pacing up and down the study. It wasn't a big room, so the lengths were quite short. I tried everything. Deep breathing exercises, quiet pep talks, loud pep talks. *Emily is going to be alright, she will recover from anorexia. Will has just broken his wrist. It's a physical injury. It will heal. Alice is just getting old. It happens to all of us. That's just life. Nothing you can do about it.* The pacing and the muttering became louder and louder. I berated myself, gave myself a good talking to. *Come on, Mark, pull yourself together. Don't be so selfish. Think about Mel, think about the kids. This is not about you. It's not your time.*

My computer still said no.

'Dad, are you alright in there?' Will asked, with a hint of concern in his voice.

'Fine, son, just doing a bit of thinking out aloud,' I called back, lying.

I was a long way off from being fine. I was beginning to catastrophise. Will sensed this and called Mel. He was worried about my weird behaviour. He wanted to know what he should do. Mel insisted I went nowhere until she got back home. She asked Will to hide the car keys. God knows what she was now thinking.

Back in my home office, I knew exactly what would happen next. The return of my broken mind meant I wouldn't be able to work anymore. The implications of not being able to work were that we wouldn't be able to afford to pay our mortgage, our bills. A full-blown agitated depression would come next, followed by months of inactivity in a desperate and unforgiving place. In the meantime, Emily would deteriorate, Alice would be left to her own devices and would quickly wither away. Will's injury wouldn't heal properly and he'd be in pain all his life. And Mel ...

It just made me shudder to think ... My head was crammed full of all this negativity and there seemed to be no way out. I knew the sequence of events. I was crystal clear how this would play out. After all, I had been here before.

But I wasn't going to go through all that misery again. I couldn't. The months and months of pain and suffering ... The mere thought of it filled me with dread.

Suddenly, I was feeling unsafe. Bad thoughts started to seep into my head.

I made an emergency call to my doctor. I told him what was going on and I asked him for an immediate referral to the Tindal Centre, the mental health facility for adults. This was the same place Mel and I had visited 12 years previously at the height of my illness. I would be safe there. I couldn't do myself any harm. The doctor made the necessary call to arrange the assessment. I called Mel to let her know. She asked me to wait until she got home so she could take me.

Drip, drip, drip, drip, drip.

Mel arrived home. She couldn't quite believe what was happening to me or how I was behaving. The summer of 2001 now flashed in front of her eyes too. Did I honestly expect her to look after

Em, Alice, and Will all on her own, and me on top of all that? And walk the dog? And manage the house? Really? She told me to pull myself together. It was an understandable reaction in the circumstances. Mel was scared. She was having her very own panic attack.

But I just couldn't pull myself together. Believe me, more than anything in the world, I wanted to. I understood all the implications, trust me I did. But I really couldn't get my act together. My mental engine was on the brink of conking out again and there seemed to be nothing I could do. I was all over the place.

Elizabeth Gilbert, best known for her 2006 memoir, *Eat, Pray, Love*, came up with the phrase, 'Embrace the glorious mess you are'.[44] At that moment in time, I was a complete mess, but I certainly didn't want to embrace myself. I am pretty sure Mel didn't either.

She drove me to the Tindal Centre. An hour previously, she had been pottering about town, doing various bits and pieces. Amazing what a difference an hour can make. As we both entered the building, another strong sense of déjà vu. The last time we were here, we both decided this was not the right place for me to be. This time, I was convinced it was the only place for me to be.

The Wonders of Lorazepam

The assessment started at half past four with a doctor I had never met. I took her through my history of depression and explained the panic I was currently in. I was completely honest about everything that had happened during the last few days. I also explained how the three possible triggers – Emily, Alice, and Will – had led to the catastrophising. I mentioned I had also experienced "fleeting suicidal thoughts" but had quickly discounted them as my family needed me. As was the case back in 2001, I remained remarkably lucid and could have been discussing the chronic lack of funding in the NHS. But my mind was in turmoil. I was just praying the doctor would look at me, turn to Mel, and confirm it was in everyone's best interests if I stayed in for a night or two. But she didn't.

She left the room briefly to discuss her diagnosis and her recommended course of action with a couple of colleagues. She came back in and prescribed me 1mg of lorazepam, an anti-anxiety tablet. I could take these up to four times a day.

I looked at her slightly incredulously. I then looked at Mel with panic in my eyes. Mel was crying.

A bloody pill! Was that it? What on earth was a pill going to do?

Back in 2001, I had been prescribed more or less every anti-depressant, every anti-anxiety tablet, every "you need help quick" tablet on the market. Nothing had ever worked. The only thing that had been effective was a 10-ton truck in Wing. I honestly didn't believe the doctor knew who or what she was dealing with. But she was convinced this was the right course of action. I certainly wasn't, but I took a little blue tablet there and then. *Here goes nothing*, I thought.

Mel and I returned home. I was leaving the safety of the harbour and returning to the wild ocean in a rubber dinghy with a leak, but without a life jacket.

A little interruption to talk about lorazepam.

It's a drug widely used to treat anxiety disorders. A common side effect is drowsiness, but not to the point where you can't operate. It is mostly used to treat fast-onset panic anxiety. But the best bit about it is that it works almost immediately. It's not like an anti-depressant you need to take for several weeks before experiencing any change.

Soon after taking it, I became a little drowsy. A nice kind of drowsy. A relaxed kind of drowsy. A "life isn't so bad after all" kind of drowsy.

When I got home, I sat and watched TV, had some supper, and took another tablet before bedtime. I slept solidly for eight hours. When I woke up the next day, I was feeling relatively relaxed, much more so than I had been during the last week, that was for sure. The signs were promising but I didn't want to take any chances. So I decided to take another tablet just in case. I felt calm and was acting normally, but the big test was still to come. My computer was waiting for me in my home study. Twenty-four hours previously, it had said no. What was it going to say this time?

I switched it on, let it boot up, waited a few anxious moments … I read a couple of emails … actioned a few things … another email … another item was ticked off the to-do list.

The computer was saying yes.

Pure, utter relief.

I got my head down and simply cracked on with things, in case the computer decided to change its mind and start shouting at me again. Admittedly, I felt a little bit drowsy, but the drowsiness was just enough to take the edge off my anxiety but not so much I wouldn't be able to concentrate on the work in front of me. I continued working for the rest of the morning. The feeling of unbridled relief continued. I took another pill at lunchtime and worked through the afternoon. I stopped working at the end of the day, turned off my computer and left my home office.

Every item had been crossed off the to-do list.

I was just so relieved. I *was* able to work after all. The day before, it appears I had simply suffered from a massive panic attack which had resulted from the gradual build-up of pressure during the last couple of weeks. A panic attack. Nothing more. My catastrophic forecasts of doom and gloom had been totally inaccurate. Yes, all the stressors were still there: Emily, Alice, Will, and work, but things didn't have to follow the same path they took back in 2001. It wasn't pre-ordained. Nothing had been written in stone. It was just a good old-fashioned panic attack.

I could have kissed that doctor at the Tindal Centre.

The next day, I went to see my GP in an almost celebratory mood and gave him the good news. He had some good news for me in return. I would be able to keep taking the lorazepam on a "need to have" basis. This meant I could keep a stash of the tablets in our bathroom cupboard and if ever I had a panic attack, I could take one to calm me down. They would always be within touching distance and because I knew they worked, and worked immediately, this provided me with peace of mind. After that period, I never needed them again, but their presence alone provided a strong placebo effect and that was good enough for me. From that point on, I would always refer to them affectionately as my "little blue friends", and they would always hold a special place both in my heart and in my cupboard.

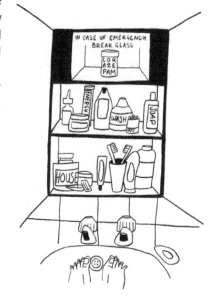

On the 17th April, I went back to the Tindal Centre to be signed off. This is how they described me in their report: *Mark was kempt and smartly dressed. There was no evidence of psychomotor agitation or retardation. There was rapport and adequate eye contact. He described his mood as upbeat and objectively, he was euthymic with some reactivity and congruent affect. He was spontaneous, and his speech was relevant and normal in rate, tone and volume. There was no functional thought disorder, hallucination or delusions elicited.*

I didn't understand many of the medical terms, but all the outward signs suggested I was okay. It had just been a temporary panic attack.

There was one other interesting element in the Tindal report. The first line read, *Mark is known to Mental Health Services with a history of anxiety.* I was amused by the wording. Rightly or wrongly, it made me sound like a petty criminal, always up to mischief and perpetually in some kind of trouble.

But for the record, I must stress that over the last 18 years, treatment of my mental health problems by all members of the NHS has been exemplary. First class. I thank each and every one of them.

So that was my little blip. In its acute stage, it didn't last longer than 12 hours, although it had been brewing for several weeks, probably several months. It taught me that you can't ever be complacent about mental health. Mental illnesses like anxiety, depression, and anorexia probably never leave you completely. They are always lurking in the undergrowth, just waiting to pounce. They always need to be treated with the utmost caution and respect.

The banisters were still in place and it was just the staircase that needed mending. They were both going to have to be extremely strong and resilient in the months ahead, as we were about to enter a new phase of increased hostilities with Ana where the battles would become longer, bloodier, and more brutal.

CHAPTER 14

THE BATTLE OF THE HIGHFIELD

(May to July 2013)

OXFORD.
CITY OF DREAMING SPIRES

When treating anorexia, particularly in the early stages, it's generally the parents who get the first shot at trying to arrest the decline and turn things around. Ideally, this happens with the help of the local CAMHS unit. The perceived wisdom is that there is a better chance of sustainable recovery if it happens within a normal home environment. In-patient stays in eating disorder clinics, under the close supervision of psychiatrists, psychologists, nutritionists, and therapists are usually the last resort.

When we got to April 2013, Mel and I hoisted the white flag and held up our hands in surrender. Ana had claimed her first victory. She was too strong for us. She knew too much. It was time for us to place Emily in the hands of the professionals, experts who knew what they were doing. That famous line from *Jaws*, the movie, comes to mind, when Roy Scheider sees the enormous size of the killer shark for the very first time and realises the scale of their task:

'You're gonna need a bigger boat.'

That bigger boat was the Highfield Adolescent Unit in Oxford, a state-of-the-art NHS facility for young people aged 11 to 18 with acute mental health needs. These are some extracts from a letter written by Emily's psychiatrist on 2nd April 2013 to the head of the Highfield Adolescent Unit:

When I met Emily with her parents, Emily appeared pale and emaciated. She is a very thin teenage girl looking younger than her age. Her hair looked dry. She described feeling dizzy and tired all the time, particularly on standing up and her blood pressure is low. Emily has been reporting very intrusive and distressing voices, some linked with her eating disorder telling her not to eat and criticising her if she has eaten anything. Emily also describes derogatory voices telling her to harm herself.

Self-harming. That was always a symptom of Emily's evil illness which really made me shudder. I couldn't fathom why anyone would want to harm themselves on purpose. Apparently, self-harmers find it difficult to express how they feel and may have detached themselves from their feelings of pain, hurt, and anger. Self-harm is one way for them to experience something physically which they are unable to experience emotionally. I wondered whether my bizarre headbanging behaviour back in 2001 was the equivalent of self-harming? Had it been my own way of trying to prove to myself I was still alive from an emotional point of view? Is feeling pain better than feeling nothing at all?

Emily's weight was now 41.3kg (91 pounds), and she had lost a total of 13kg (29 pounds) since her initial assessment the previous December. That represented a 21% weight deficit. Although her BMI was now hovering around the 16 mark (remember, 18.5 is the minimum healthy mark), that wasn't considered low enough to be admitted as an in-patient. Somewhat ironically, to get a bed, your weight and BMI needed to be so low and your condition so acute that you were almost at death's door. There just weren't enough beds available for this illness. In economic terms, demand was outstripping supply. This meant the most serious cases were always the priority.

Emily was admitted as a day patient at the Highfield at the beginning of May, as much for her deteriorating mood as for her declining weight.

As a result, Mel and I had to get used to a new daily routine. One of us would set our alarms for six o'clock in the morning Monday through to Saturday, to drive a sleepy Emily to Oxford, where she would have breakfast at half past seven. It was a two-hour round trip. Every evening, we would return to the Unit at seven o'clock, collect our punch-drunk daughter after she had finished her evening meal and bring her home for her final snack of the day. Sunday was our "day off" when everybody could have a lie-in.

I was still working flat-out at the time. If Mel needed to be at school with Jack, I would take on the extra burden of one or more of the Oxford legs on top of my work diary. Those days were very long.

The Highfield Unit was a high security building with a coded entry system, cameras everywhere, and a high staff-to-patient ratio. During the treatment period, you were locked inside for the duration of the day. There was time and space for socialising as well as a strong focus on rehabilitation and re-education around nutrition. But more than anything else the Highfield was where you went to eat ... and regain weight. Scientifically precise meal plans were provided for each of the young patients based on their age, height, and weight. They were nutritiously well balanced and, critically, packed full of enough calories to bring about weight gain.

A strict activity timetable had been established and levels of physical exertion were closely measured and monitored. The lower the person's weight, the less activity they were allowed. At one end of the spectrum, where the weight deficit was at least 40% lower than the healthy target, there was complete bed rest and meals were served in your room. Solitary confinement. As weight was gradually restored, levels of activity were slowly increased, and when weight was close to being fully restored, moderate activities like swimming and walking were permitted again.

SURELY ANA DIDN'T HAVE AN ANSWER TO ALL THIS

This was a superb institution with outstanding facilities. It was staffed with psychologists, psychiatrists, nutritionists, and counsellors, all trained in the treatment of eating disorders and all completely familiar with Ana's little tricks. Emily was in the hands of experts at last.

We were going to be okay.

The Animals Arrive One by One

The parents were also given support and guidance on how to deal with the illness. A well-renowned psychologist in the field of eating disorders, Dr Janet Treasure, had developed a powerful analogy based on different animals to help parents deal with their disordered children when they were at home. Her animal analogy was widely embraced in the world of therapy because the parent was often the one stakeholder with most influence on the recovery process of the sufferer. The better skilled they were as counsellors, therapists, and supporters, the better chances their children had of making a recovery.

Mel and I had failed miserably during the first six months of the illness, so we were thankful for any help we could get. Even from a bunch of random animals.

Here is a short summary of the animals and the parental behaviours they represent, both unhelpful and helpful:

Jellyfish. They show too much emotion and therefore exhibit too little control over proceedings. They are unable to hide their distress and anger at what is happening around them. Stings occur because their uncontrolled and raw emotions are often mirrored by outbursts from the sufferer themselves.

Ostriches. They exhibit an avoidance of emotion. They live in denial because they find it too hard to cope with what is going on right in front of them. They prefer to bury their head in the sand and pretend nothing is happening. As a result, the sufferer sees the carer as uncaring and feels unloved. Their self-esteem ebbs away further still.

Kangaroos. They are the complete opposite to Ostriches. They treat the sufferer with kid gloves, mollycoddle them, and let them jump into the kangaroo pouch at every opportunity to avoid any difficult conversations. This cocoon-like existence prevents the child from tackling the illness and addressing the challenges they are faced with.

Rhinos. They use brute force, logic, and strong arguments to try to convince the sufferer their way is the right way. This often leads to confrontation and only serves to strengthen Ana's resolve further still. If you start hurling grenades her way, she summons the rest of her army to return fire with even heavier artillery.

Terriers. Their chief attribute is never-ending persistence. They have the same objective as Rhinos but try to achieve this in a cajoling, nagging, irritating kind of way. After a while, the sufferer tunes out, blocks out the noise, and stops listening. Ana learns to bark back even more loudly and more annoyingly, and nothing is achieved.

The two role model animals are the Dolphin and the St Bernard Dog. They demonstrate the right behaviours when tackling anorexia, ones proven to help rather than hinder recovery.

Dolphins. Their strategy is to use just enough caring and control to help nudge the sufferer towards recovery. Imagine your child is out at sea, wearing a life vest and the life vest is Ana. She is struggling and suffering but she is afloat, and without the life vest / Ana, she fears she will drown. The Dolphin persuades the sufferer to take off their life vest and start swimming back towards the shore. They promise to remain by their side, encouraging, supporting, loving, demonstrating that life without Ana is both possible and preferable.

St Bernard. They provide compassion as well as consistency. They try to instil the hope in your loved one that the situation can and will change. They are forever the optimist and show nothing but kindness and love. They remain unflappable even in times of trouble, and most important of all, they never, ever, leave your side.

The theory underpinning the animal analogy was spot on, and the theorist in me loved the thinking. It couldn't be faulted, and Mel and I tried our best to be Dolphins and St Bernards. We would leave those sessions positively barking and making sweet squeaking Dolphin noises on our way home. We were desperate to kick our Jellyfish, Ostrich, Kangaroo, Rhino, and Terrier tendencies into touch. However, when the pressure was on, we inevitably reverted back to these destructive traits in some form or other. We knew full well we had to be either Dolphins or St Bernards, but when your daughter is hiding stuff, lying to you, being rude to you, and throwing her life away in front of your very eyes, it's hard to translate theory into practice.

As a management trainer, I knew this pattern of behaviour only too well. Students would often leave my workshops and courses, brimming full of new ideas, determined to change how they did things back in the workplace. But when they got back to their desks and were confronted with 350 unread emails and an unsympathetic, impatient boss, all of their good intentions would usually fly out of the window.

Habits always die hard, particularly bad ones.

And Ana was such a strong and powerful enemy. Even worse, she had now been joined by all the other evil little Anas in the Highfield. She had loyal allies. They had all come together to form Ana's Army and they were now sharing all their dirty little tactics and secrets with one another. Ana had even managed to infiltrate the zoo and get under the skin of the Jellyfish, the Ostriches, the Kangaroos, the Rhinos, and the Terriers. She was whipping them up into a frenzy.

The Dolphin and the poor St Bernard just didn't stand a chance.

ANA RAN A BRUTAL TRAINING CAMP

All the highly trained staff at the Highfield were excellent. They really were. They did everything within their power to help Emily fight her Ana. Like Mel and me during the early skirmishes, they had given it their best shot. But throughout her time in Oxford, Emily remained frustratingly close to Ana and they were now closer than they had ever been before. They were identical twins, joined at the hip, impossible to tell apart. Ana kept persuading her sister that if she stayed close and did what she told her to do, then she would be okay. Unfortunately for us, Emily still believed in her.

There was always one overriding and frightening message from the professionals: until a sufferer of anorexia is ready to get better and prepared to let go of their Ana, there is absolutely nothing anybody else can really do to help, however professional, knowledgeable or skilful they might be.

Emily just wasn't ready to do that yet.

So on the 22nd of July, almost two and a half months after being admitted as a day patient, and just under 200 two-hour round trips to and from Oxford, our damaged daughter was discharged from the Highfield Unit. Her weight was now exactly the same as it had been on arrival – 41kg (90 pounds). Mel and I felt disappointed and deflated. We had placed so much hope in the Highfield and had invested so much of our time and energy. There had been no progress.

In fact, Emily had gone backwards and Ana had become stronger.

The Battle of Highfield had been lost. Without doubt, it had been a difficult time for Mel and me, but the one consolation of this period was that it allowed us both to get on with regular stuff between the hours of nine in the morning and six o'clock in the evening while our daughter was in safe hands in Oxford. I was able to crack on with the regular freelance work I was getting from both Brand Learning and Imparta. That was a relief. At this point, Creative Creatures remained deep in hibernation. My brain still wasn't in the mood for any of Einstein's clever stuff.

The positive news was that my mental defences were still holding firm and there was no sign of either the little blip or Big Blip making an unwanted return. The bad news was my mother was now deteriorating week by week and would be requiring more attention and closer supervision from both Mel and me.

Emily would be requiring the same back home in Stewkley.

The pressure was now back on.

The Ceasefire Agreement

Before leaving the Highfield, we had one last meeting with the professionals at the unit who had been responsible for Emily during her time there. This was the formal discharge meeting where we would discuss and agree the rules of engagement back in the community. It was a negotiation of sorts.

NEGOTIATION TABLE

At the meeting, it was agreed by all parties that the initial objective was to help Emily maintain her current weight in the community. Not increase or allow to decrease but maintain. This was the all-important clause in the agreement. Once Emily was able to maintain her weight, we would then consider moving on to a weight-increase plan. In order to achieve this goal, Emily agreed to stay around family members an hour after meals, but in return, she would be allowed to move around the house and garden during this time, and this would still happen under supervision.

Another concession was that our daughter would be allowed to prepare some of her own meals, but always under the watchful eye of either Mel or me. She agreed to be weighed weekly at a neutral venue and to have her blood pressure monitored periodically. She also agreed to ongoing individual therapy, including some sessions on mindfulness to help build up confidence levels both in herself and in others around her. She was no longer the popular, bubbly Emily we once knew. She was a pale imitation of her former self, physically and mentally.

Mel and I found that soul-destroying.

These were the terms of the ceasefire deal. The appeasement. In short, we will give you more freedom and latitude around eating, we won't put any more pressure on you to gain weight. Your side of the bargain is that you agree not to lose any more.

But even back then, I had my strong suspicions that some secret plot was being hatched. I could imagine Ana convincing Emily it was now time to get out of the Highfield. It was probably getting too tough in there, not much fun, and they needed an escape plan. While everybody was happily signing the discharge agreement, my bet is that Ana was already two steps ahead of us.

Emily Puts on Weight

Before Emily was discharged from the Highfield, she was given a detailed meal plan to follow. This itemised precisely what she needed to eat for three main meals and three snacks every day. We were able to work out how this translated into a daily calorie figure which was 2,200. This was what was required to maintain weight. In the unit, she had been on a much higher amount during her three and a half month stay, but with the help of Ana and her army, had succeeded in beating the system and keeping her weight down.

During her first three days back home, we recorded exactly what Emily ate, working out the calorie count meticulously at the end of every day. The totals were as follows: Sunday – 1,568 calories; Monday – 1,549 calories; Tuesday – 1,626 calories. She was already 600 calories short of what she needed to eat to maintain weight. The appeasement deal was already under pressure, and the arguments started once again. We were convinced Emily would be losing weight in no time at all. Dolphin and St Bernard soon became Rhino and Terrier, as the temperature started to rise in the house.

Emily and Ana were not sticking to their side of the deal. It was collapsing before it had even started.

And then a remarkable thing happened. That Thursday, I was running a workshop for Unilever up in the north of England, when I got a text from Mel, mid-morning, asking me to call her urgently. When I spoke to her, she said Emily had been weighed that morning and her weight had gone up by 2kg (4.5 pounds). Two kilograms! That was unheard of. I screamed out loud in celebration down the phone. Emily's weight had finally increased. Amazing news!

My joy was short-lived, however, when Mel told me Emily was distraught at the news of the unexpected increase. She wasn't talking to anybody. According to our daughter, her weight was not supposed to go up. *That wasn't part of the "deal". It said quite clearly in the contract, in black and white, that she was supposed to be on a maintenance plan and not a weight-gain plan. What the hell was happening, she was asking?*

As I got off the phone to resume my workshop, I wasn't sure what to think or feel. I was totally confused myself because the weight gain should not have happened. It didn't make any sense. The rule of thumb is that to put on a pound of weight, you need to eat an extra 500 calories a day for a week. To put on just over four pounds, Emily would have to have eaten between 4,000 and 4,500 calories a day. That had definitely not happened. There were only two possible explanations, one possible, the other probable.

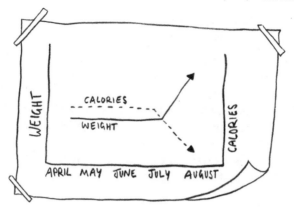

THE GRAPH THAT MADE NO SENSE

The possibility first. Sometimes, unexpected weight gains or losses do happen for biological reasons that nobody quite understands. The body doesn't always react logically to either an increased or reduced intake in food. That is why eating disorder specialists tend to take the average weight across two or three weeks in order to iron out the anomalies and get an accurate picture of the true situation. This could feasibly have happened to Emily that day as God only knew what her body was thinking anymore.

The other explanation was more probable and more sinister. Ana wanted an excuse to scupper the deal that had been brokered a few days previously. Therefore, she could have persuaded Emily to water load massively before the weigh-in, either the night before or first thing in the morning. The scales would have shot up as Emily stepped on to them, but the reading would have been false and misleading. Carrying extra water to put on weight doesn't count. That's cheating, but it gave the twins the way out they were looking for.

I finished off the workshop and on the three-hour train trip down south I was still thinking about the mystery of the unexpected weight increase and planning how I was going to deal with a disappointed daughter. No rest for the wicked.

When I got back home that evening, Emily was sitting curled up in the corner of her bedroom, still disconsolate, still angry. 'We had a deal, Dad. We all signed off on the deal. You haven't kept your side of the bargain.' I really wasn't quite sure whether I was talking to my daughter or to her twin sister. Was Emily genuinely upset? Confused? Or was she simply play acting? No idea at all. I was tired and didn't want to think about it anymore. As I left the room, I almost wished I was going back up north.

The next day, Emily and Ana proceeded to rip up the agreement. The ceasefire had lasted just under a week. It was now in tatters.

The twins went on the rampage for the next few weeks. They restricted their meal plan to an intake of 1,000 calories a day, and there was no discussion or debate with anybody. Nothing either Mel or I said had the slightest impact on what they did. It didn't matter which animal behaviours we adopted, and so for a while we simply gave up trying to intervene.

In fact, that's not strictly true.

If you want to know which animal we mirrored most closely during that time, it was probably the Lemming, 'a member of a crowd with no originality or voice of his own. One who speaks or repeats only what he has been told. A tool. A cretin.'... according to the Urban Dictionary.[45]

Yes, Mel and I had become a pair of useless Lemmings.

Two things then happened during the next few weeks. Firstly, and unsurprisingly, Emily's weight began to head south once again, and she started losing an average of 1kg (2.2 pounds) per week. It had now dipped below the 40kg (88 pounds) mark for the first time.

The second thing that happened was Emily's mood experienced a remarkable transformation. Now that she was in complete control of what she ate and drank, our daughter was as happy as we had seen her for almost eight months. She was chatting and joking, being civil with her parents, going on shopping trips to London with girlfriends. She was now doing everything a normal 17-year-old should be doing except one thing: she wasn't eating enough. She was experiencing what is known in the eating disorder world as an "anorexia high", a state of mind not dissimilar to what you get when you take ecstasy.

Valerie Compan at the Centre National de la Recherche Scientifique (CNRS) in France is one of the growing number of researchers who believe anorexia works in the same way as any drug addiction does. Sufferers can become "hooked" on the feeling of self-control they get by restricting their food intake. By conducting experiments on mice, Compan found that both anorexia and ecstasy use activate some of the same brain pathways, concluding that starving yourself can become addictive. And with addiction comes pleasure, even though it may only be short term.[46]

Should we have been harder with Emily? Should we have put our foot down more, refused her any of her privileges? Or were we right to allow her a taste of normality, in the hope she might realise what life could be like if she found the strength to get better? *Erm, pass. I really don't know.*

Each and every day, Mel and I were being asked to make tactical decisions that felt like the right course of action at the time. We were under no illusion that we didn't always make the right call, but Emily always held the trump card. If pushed too far, she could always threaten to do the one thing that terrified us more than anything else.

Stop eating completely.

So, during the month of August, there were both positives and negatives. The positives were there were no longer any major arguments in the Simmonds household. Emily was happy doing what she wanted when she wanted, with very little input or interference from the two Lemmings. The house was calmer now, less of a battlefield. The negative was that our daughter was slowly starving herself to death. She was dancing her way merrily into oblivion.

What a difference a year can make. Twelve months previously, we had been celebrating the successes of the British Olympic and Paralympic teams in London. We had been raising our glasses to toast the golden decade that had just finished. It had scored 8.5 out of 10. I had scored 33 out of 40 on my work / life business plan. A few tweaks were required here and there, but nothing major.

However, I had worked in the business environment long enough to know that all plans change. Nothing is ever fixed. No company can ever be totally in control of external factors which change from one year to the next. Plans need to be continually updated and flexed. The 2003–2012 one was already a relic.

The status quo in the late summer of 2013 couldn't go on any longer. We needed to stop being useless Lemmings and Ostriches with our heads buried deep in the sand. We had to do something quick to arrest Emily's decline. We had now given up hope she would be able to restart her A Levels, even though she had been offered a place at a new school for September. All the interventions to date had failed and her weight was plummeting at a rate of knots. We would have to get our thinking caps on and come up with something new before it was too late.

So, I took some time off work and planned to spend the next two weeks in front of my computer at home.

We were in urgent need of yet another plan.

CHAPTER 15

THE CARDINAL CLINIC CRUSADES

(August 2013 to March 2014)

JUNGLE WARFARE JUST OUTSIDE
ROYAL WINDSOR

A little diversion. In March 2013, Will, our eldest, had broken his wrist badly five minutes before the end of a rugby match. My heart sank as I saw him being stretchered off the pitch and bundled into an ambulance. Fortunately for us, the Leicester Royal Infirmary was only five minutes away from the ground, so it wasn't long before we were in Accident & Emergency.

One week later, Will went under the knife at our local hospital. The operation was due to last two hours. It lasted six. When the doctor emerged from surgery, he was sweating profusely. He confessed that it was one of the trickiest wrist injuries he had ever operated on. Apparently, there were so many bone fragments floating around, it was like putting together a 500-piece jigsaw.

Six months later, after several more consultations with the surgeon, and numerous physiotherapy sessions to strengthen the wrist, Will was free of pain and started playing rugby again at Manchester University.

The point of the little diversion is this: Will had suffered a serious injury and the recovery process was relatively long, complicated, and arduous. But at least there was a clearly defined path to follow. Nobody was stumbling around in the dark, wondering what to do next. You knew that if you did X, Y would probably happen. There was a step-by-step manual available.

Unfortunately, this wasn't the case with Emily. When she developed anorexia, we went to the GP who promptly referred us to the CAMHS unit. They in turn helped us try to manage the illness at home. When this didn't work out, we agreed that Emily would attend the Highfield Unit as a day patient. When Emily failed to make any progress there, she came back home ... Then what? No idea.

This is where the manual ended. She had already failed to make any headway under our supervision at the beginning of 2013. What were we supposed to do now? Emily's weight was still not low enough to be considered acute, so we couldn't apply for a bed at an NHS eating disorder clinic. The Highfield were unlikely to have her back due to her unwillingness to engage with the programme. What was the next option in the recovery process? Who should we turn to? Whose point of view should we trust? It was just like in 2001 when I was so ill, and I desperately needed black and white but all I could ever get was the in-between grey.

Mel and I had to make the next decision ourselves that August, as Emily's weight continued to freefall. From this point on, we were clutching at straws, making best guesses. We decided she needed an in-patient stay somewhere and that somewhere had to be a private clinic. Fortunately, we had a private healthcare scheme, and, equally as fortunately, there was some provision in it for psychiatric in-patient treatment. I checked whether Emily would be covered under the terms of the policy. She was. We had 45 days of in-patient stay at our disposal.

First big sigh of relief.

Hunting for the Right Person and the Right Place

I then proceeded to spend my "summer vacation" head down in my home office either on the phone or on my computer. My task was to find the one person and the one institution to whom I would "award" those precious BUPA days to help turn our daughter's illness around. Forty-five days was the maximum amount of time the policy allowed. I had one shot at it, so I had to get it right.

The tricky bit was there was no clear guidance to help me make the right choice. It would have been helpful if there had been the equivalent of league tables that publicised success rates for major examinations at different schools. I needed to know which psychiatrist out there was best qualified. Who really understood anorexia better than anyone else? Who had a track record of helping anorexics recover? What was their success rate? You'd think there would be a table that listed the top 20 specialists in eating disorders in the UK, based on performance and results. But there wasn't. It was just down to me to trawl through every clinic's website, study every doctor's profile, look at the evidence available to help me select the right person.

SAME OFFICE DIFFERENT WALLS

It was like a business simulation. You have a clear objective (in my case, find the best qualified doctor). You are given little or no guidance on how to achieve this. You have limited access to any relevant information. You need to make up your own process for selection, and you are encouraged to use both your head and heart to make the correct decision: a combination of hard data and gut feel. And on top of that, you only have two weeks to complete the exercise. This was my brief. The only difference between a business game and what I was doing that August was the size of the prize. It wasn't a box of chocolates or a crate of beer that was up for grabs for the winning solution. It was my daughter's life.

After a couple of weeks of searching the internet and conducting several telephone interviews to get down to a shortlist, I felt that I had found the right person and the right place. The "successful candidate" trained in General Psychiatry in London (Charing Cross and St George's Hospitals). She held an NHS Consultant post in Berkshire working in acute psychiatry and in eating disorders and had set up a comprehensive specialist eating disorders service for Berkshire. She had published widely in this area of psychiatry and was currently the medical director at the Cardinal Clinic, just outside Windsor.

Mel and I wanted to meet the director and see the place for ourselves before mentioning anything to Emily. At that time, she seemed to be having such a good time losing weight in Stewkley that we had no idea how she would react to the prospect of an in-patient stay when all the fun would stop in an instant.

The Cardinal Clinic is a private psychiatric clinic set in beautiful grounds on the outskirts of Windsor. First opened in October 1976, it deals with all aspects of mental health from depression and drug abuse to alcoholism and anger management. Patients are first seen for an assessment with one of the consultant psychiatrists who identify the issues that need addressing. If required, a personalised and structured treatment approach is tailored to meet the patient's specific requirements. In-patients have their own individual bedrooms, some single and some double, all with en-suite bathrooms.[47]

The two advantages the Cardinal Clinic had over the Highfield Unit were firstly the other in-patients were generally older than Emily and the majority had admitted themselves voluntarily. They were mature adults from all walks of life who were committed to getting better. Mel and I hoped one or two might become surrogate mothers or fathers and help steer Emily in the right direction, even though they would have problems of their own to deal with. And secondly, a variety of different mental health disorders were being treated at the Cardinal, not just anorexia. This meant there weren't going to be a couple of dozen other nasty little Anas running around, trying to form another battalion of Ana's Army. If Emily's Ana wanted to succeed at the Cardinal, she would have to deploy new tactics and strategies. She would be forced to adapt her approach and operate stealthily, more like a lone wolf.

We felt it was the right place for our very sick daughter, but would she think the same? Emily had reached rock bottom and even though she had experienced the thrill of an anorexic high throughout August, she still had the presence of mind to realise just how very ill she was. She was under no illusion about how tough the regime at the Cardinal would be, but she was convinced she was now up for the challenge. Having met the medical director and her excellent team, we were sure that she was now in good hands. We were confident that we had selected wisely. Fortunately, Emily thought so too.

She was admitted to the Cardinal Clinic in the last week of August. As Mel and I enjoyed a glass of wine after returning home that evening, we experienced two quite contrasting emotions. Firstly, there was undoubtedly an immense feeling of sadness. We had a very sick daughter who now weighed around 37kg (82 pounds). During her assessment, the medical director had been shocked just how ill she was and was adamant she needed urgent treatment. It was hard to believe that just 12 months previously, Emily was about to begin sixth form with her whole life in front of her.

A HOUSE WITHOUT ANA

And secondly, Mel and I would both be lying if we didn't admit to feeling a sense of relief. We wouldn't have to put up with Ana's company in our house for a few weeks and witness, first hand, what she was doing to Emily. We could get on with our lives once again, in the full knowledge that our daughter was being expertly looked after. For the next two months, our thoughts would never be far away from her and we would visit her every few days or so, but at long last we had some breathing space, a little bit of distance between us and the illness.

Solitary Confinement

Having spent the first few days adjusting to her new surroundings, getting to know the other in-patients, and learning the ropes and routines, Emily was unexpectedly whisked away and put into "solitary confinement" for 24 hours, 7 days a week. In other words, she was confined to her bedroom.

She had been refusing food already. The view was that Emily's health was not going to improve quickly enough if she remained in contact with the other patients around her as well as with her friends on social media. They would be a distraction. So both privileges were removed. Emily had to learn how to "sit with her illness", fight it by confronting it within the confines of the four walls of her bedroom. She was being pitted directly against Ana and being asked to face her demons head on. At one level, it just seemed cruel. Emily had been sold the benefits of the Cardinal during her assessment visit and solitary confinement was not one of them. On the other hand, we understood the logic behind the clinic's approach, and we trusted their judgement completely. Anything that might break the deadlock had to be tried.

For the next month, Emily hardly left her room. She took every one of her six meals in her cosy bedroom, accompanied by one of the very patient nurses. She was weighed twice a week and the incentive to put on weight was that the quicker she did this, the sooner she would get released back into the mainstream of the clinic. However, during the first couple of weeks, Emily found it impossible to gain weight. Her starting point was 37.9kg (84 pounds) and it no more than trickled upwards. Her bathroom remained locked, so no possibility of purging. No obvious hiding places anywhere. We had no idea what was happening and why the pounds weren't piling on.

Ana was very good. In fact, she was a magician.

Emily was still 10kg (22 pounds) short of the minimum healthy BMI. Just a few weeks of BUPA funding were left. We still had a long way to go.

There are two problems when your weight remains low for long periods of time. The first is physical. People like Emily will invariably stop having periods which significantly increases the risk of developing osteoporosis. This is a serious condition that weakens bones and makes them more likely to break.[48] Emily had long since stopped having her periods.

The second problem is emotional. By effectively starving your brain of the nutrition it requires, you limit its capacity to process information and think rationally. As far as Emily was concerned, her continued reluctance or inability to gain weight at the Cardinal meant any form of talking therapy wasn't much more than a waste of time. It was like filling a barrel with expensive wine only to find it had a big hole in it. So Emily was excluded from all the various classes like "coping with anxiety and depression" and "dealing with body image" because her brain was that barrel.

During the weeks spent in almost complete isolation, Emily would entertain herself by becoming immersed in the creative arts. Drawing, painting, writing poems and short stories, learning how to play the guitar.

Art therapy was a well-established technique used to help mental health sufferers enjoy some calm and peace, find ways of expressing their inner turmoil, and quieten their often chaotic minds. Emily discovered a real passion for art she had never shown before. It had never been a pastime she had ever expressed any real interest in. Whenever she showed us a piece of

ANA WAS FINALLY GETTING A PROLONGED TASTE OF HER OWN MEDICINE

work she had created during the day, Mel and I always felt proud she was at least doing something constructive with her endless hours of free time. But it was always accompanied by a feeling of hidden disappointment and sadness this was happening in a clinic and not at school.

However, the subject matter of her art or poetry wasn't ever sun-drenched beaches or beautiful landscapes. It always explored the dark side of life that mirrored the turmoil in her head. One poem she wrote, more than anything we ever read in any book or article, proved to us what a brutal and unforgiving illness anorexia was.

Emily lived with Ana all day and all night long. Ana had succeeded in infiltrating our daughter's mind, body, and soul like an alien looking for a new home to inhabit. She had proved herself time and time again to be a really nasty piece of work. The irony was that Emily knew precisely what Ana was trying to do to her but found herself powerless to do anything about it. She was wedded to the devil.

I was visited by a stranger today
by Emily Simmonds

I was visited by a stranger today,
she called herself Ana and requested to stay.

How long I asked?
But she would not say.

At first she was polite, easy company.
Never demanded anything, pretty strange, you see.

Strange because she required no bed,
and never once asked if she could be fed.

I'd offer her breakfast, but she'd always decline;
'A glass of water, that'll be fine.'

'Any lunch or dinner?' I'd continue to ask,
'I'm so full from breakfast, I think I will pass.'

This soon became uncomfortable for me.
A feeling arose in my stomach; I felt so guilty!

It felt so strange that there we both sat,
only me with my sandwich ... I just felt so fat.

My quiet guest Ana suddenly spoke up.
She had ideas and plans that would help 'cheer me up'

She said she could make me feel happy and strong,
that the guilt would just vanish, I could do nothing wrong.

She said I'd be perfect and right there you see,
that word is how Ana gained trust from me.

I asked how long she was able to stay:
'For you, my new friend, every single day.'

Her plan was straight-forward, an easy target to meet:
each day, I'd simply avoid food - just not eat.

Ana lived in my mind to help me resist,
to block out hunger from meals I'd missed.

'You're worthless and fat', she would say to me,
but it was all part of her plan to stop me eating, you see.

Her tactics were ruthless and by the words that she said,
I believed that I didn't deserve to be fed.

The worst thing of all was the lies that I told.
Ana never showed mercy, always said to be bold.

②

'Act!' she'd say, 'and convince them you've eaten!'
Backing down wasn't an option, she wouldn't be beaten.

She was sharp and creative with more than one trick:
Hiding food, over-exercising and, of course, being sick.

Ana's methods were extreme, they were agonisingly cruel.
She ruined my education and friendships at school.

Destroying my family was her most evil play.
I just hope that my parents will forgive me some day.

'Please Ana, when will you go?' I'd say
'I cannot leave now, you need me to stay!'

She restricted my diet and the less that I ate,
The quicker and easier it became to lose weight.

Ana played with my mind; 'Em, you're not even ill.'
Knowing these lies that she told had the powers to kill.

I became tired and weak; all movements were slower.
My mind started to break as my mood became lower.

So down and depressed, without any faith or hope,
I tried to end it all. I just couldn't cope.

③

My weight dropped so quickly - from 8 to 5 stone.
I wasn't Emily anymore, I was a shell; skin and bone.

Only then did I realise that I'd been such a fool.
Ana never wanted my happiness, she was no friend at all.

Her goal became clear, what she really wanted of me:
To starve me to death like a true enemy.

So here I am, in a clinic getting help that I need.
I won't lie, it's a struggle, but I'm determined to succeed.

I'm going to beat this thing that wished me dead.
Remove Ana from my life and kick her out of my head.

I was visited by a stranger that day.
Her name: 'Anorexia Nervosa', and I let her stay.

So please, if Ana visits you in a similar way.
Think of me, turn your back, and just walk, walk away.

④

206

We hoped that solitary confinement was the answer to all our prayers, painful though it was for Emily. This period must have been even more painful for Ana. She would have been bored out of her mind watching Emily find her creative streak, listening to her dodgy chords, watching paint dry.

Good. She deserved it.

Either Mel or I would visit Emily at weekends. Instead of heading west to Oxford, we were now heading south to Windsor. And when we couldn't get there, Emily's dutiful grandfather, who lived locally, would come and sit with her in her room or in the clinic garden. The benefit to Emily when we visited, aside from seeing her family, was that she was granted parole for an hour or so. As long as she was wrapped up in a warm blanket, we could escort her outside the building to breathe in some fresh air and enjoy the manicured grounds. The other condition of her parole was that we had to take her out in a wheelchair. The clinic was adamant Emily wasn't to take any exercise of any form during this first stage of the recovery process.

Losing a calorie was always so much easier than gaining one.

Little by little, Emily's weight started to increase ... 39.6kg (87 pounds) ... 40.0 (88) ... 40.8 (90) ... This was painfully slow progress but eventually it meant she now found herself in a better position to negotiate a permanent release. As a result of her hard-won weight gains, Emily was allowed to join the other in-patients in the clinic both at mealtimes and during the various therapy classes. This was her first small victory. It also gave the three of us the chance to get to know some of the other interesting residents being treated.

A compassionate finance director who had been working out in Hong Kong for one of the Big Four accountancy firms, an HR director, a make-up artist, a footballer, an ex-diplomat, a Cambridge University undergraduate ... an array of individuals each with their own unique story to tell. All ages too, from 17

(Emily, who was the youngest) up to and beyond 60. I must admit I had hoped there was a point at which mental illness would retire just like the rest of us. I found it dispiriting to think that nobody was exempt.

The range of mental illnesses they were being treated for included anxiety, depression, drug and alcohol addiction, OCD, post-traumatic stress disorder, as well as both anorexia and bulimia. When I talked to the other patients, I couldn't help but wonder whether the Cardinal might have been right for me all those years ago. A change of environment that could have alleviated my desperate situation and shortened my Big Blip?

I was struck by the "I'm just so tired of life" looks on the faces, the dead eyes and furrowed brows. A part of me just wanted to hug them and tell them it was going to be okay. They just needed to hang on. Believe there was light at the end of the tunnel. But they just couldn't see it yet. I knew that.

BUPA Friday

The two main advantages of Emily putting on weight were firstly she would become stronger both physically and emotionally. On a practical level, as far as Mel and I were concerned, there was one other very important reason why Emily's weight needed to go up. Ongoing BUPA medical insurance funding was dependent on it.

Although in theory Emily had 45 days of in-patient treatment under the terms of the policy, she would only be granted her full entitlement if there was visible and tangible progress. In other words, she needed to put on weight every week before BUPA would sign off the next tranche of payment. Or at least show some concrete signs that weight increase was on the cards sometime soon. On one hand, you could understand the logic. If an expensive treatment is not working, then there is little point paying for it to continue. On another, it felt quite harsh. Mental health doesn't work in straight lines and the recovery process is bound to be a bumpy road. It's a real Snakes and Ladders experience where there will always be as many of the latter as there will be of the former.

The funding issue was a very stressful experience for Mel and me. Every Thursday, Emily would get weighed and the clinic would then submit a report to BUPA. This would include her weight as well as some commentary on how she was progressing. Every Friday morning, BUPA would be called to find out whether they were prepared to continue paying for treatment. The clinic would then call us to give us the news. If BUPA had refused to continue, we would have had to make a choice. Either take Emily out of the

EVERYTHING WAS
CROSSED FOR THE
CALL ON BUPA FRIDAY

clinic or fund her stay ourselves. On average, the weekly cost of a private bed is anywhere between £3,500 and £5,000.

Fortunately for us, and despite Emily's painfully snail-like progress, BUPA always said yes.

Emily is Still Not Ready to Recover

Towards the end of October 2013, just under seven weeks after entering the Cardinal, our BUPA funding ran out. The 45 days were up. Emily's weight had started to inch upwards at a snail's pace. To Mel and me, it seemed leaving the clinic at that junction would have been premature. We were trying very hard to convince ourselves she was on the brink of a big breakthrough. We thought long and hard before deciding we would raid our savings and find two weeks' worth of additional funding. If the weight could just go up by another few pounds, it would give her a much better chance of surviving life "on the outside".

Two weeks later Emily's weight had still not budged. It was still only 41.9kg (92 pounds). She had put on 4kg (9 pounds) in just under nine weeks. The target weight increase for somebody staying in a clinic under 24-hour supervision is 1kg (2.2 pounds) a week. Emily had achieved half of that. If things had gone to plan, she would not have been too far off the minimum healthy BMI target. As it was, she was still 6kg (13 pounds) short.

The team of psychiatrists, psychologists, nutritionists, therapists, and carers had done their absolute best to help Emily recover. I could not find fault in anything, either the people or the place. The problem was that Emily was still joined at the hip to Ana and all attempts to prise them apart had ultimately been unsuccessful.

A very small part of me took my hat off to Ana. I admired her. I have no idea how she had done it, how she'd managed to prevent our daughter from making significant progress. Emily was kept under the closest of close supervision for almost eight weeks. The team did everything humanly possible to loosen Ana's grip on our daughter and drive her out of our lives. But, somehow, Ana survived in the woodland environment of the Cardinal and she soon learnt how to thrive. She was always "lurking in the bushes" somewhere, exerting her ever-increasing influence over Emily. She may well have left our home in Stewkley, but she seemed equally at home just outside Royal Windsor.

The clinic was very open and honest with us. In their opinion, Emily was still not ready to recover and until she was, there really was no point in continuing her sojourn there. She needed to go away, take a "holiday" from the clinic, and when she felt ready to recommence the battle with Ana, they would then be prepared to re-consider further treatment.

It was a painful decision to hear, but it was the correct one.

No-man's Land

The definition of no-man's land is 'An area of land that is not owned or controlled by anyone, for example the area of land between two opposing armies.'[49] During the next four months, we found ourselves stuck in no-man's land. We didn't want to push things too hard just in case Ana struck back even harder. Ana probably didn't fancy a return to solitary confinement either,

so she agreed to lay down her weapons for a while. It felt as if we were all in limbo.

When Emily left the Cardinal at the end of October, her weight was 41.6kg (92 pounds), hovering just above a BMI level of 16. She was not in any acute danger, but her body and mind were both still unhealthy. She came back home to Stewkley and almost immediately found part-time work in a local café and a country pub. She needed to get out of the house as much as possible, because home now felt more and more like a prison to her. It held too many bad memories. By working, at least she would get the opportunity to meet ordinary people in normal environments. And again, we just hoped that a taste of normality would make her realise what she was missing.

She had also had enough of clinic life for a while.

Mel and I took a breather. We were not quite sure what was supposed to happen next, so we just plodded along. We kept an eye on our daughter, monitored her weight, but that was about it. Christmas 2013 came and went, and before we knew it, it was 2014.

I have very little memory of work during this time. I was still working, for sure, getting enough freelance work to pay the bills, but it remains just one big blur. Days became weeks and weeks became months.

Just one long blur.

By this time, our attention had been diverted away from Emily and towards Alice, my mother. The previous September, she had been diagnosed with terminal lung cancer and she had spent the last few months in a nursing home, just north of Aylesbury. She passed away peacefully and fairly painlessly on 14th January. During the last year of her life, she had become a source of strength and support to Emily. Whenever our daughter was at home, she would always go and visit Alice in the village, open up and share her darkest thoughts and feelings. Alice just listened, encouraged, and loved. She never judged. She knew the score. She had been to the darkest of dark places herself, so she always picked the right words and the right way in which to say them. I had always hoped Emily could have found the strength to recover during Alice's lifetime, but that wasn't to be.

Ana didn't do sentimentality.

Everybody loved Alice, none more so than Emily. They were a couple of peas in a pod who "got" one another, even though they were two generations apart. They developed a special bond in the same way my mother did with everyone around her. Alice's death hit Emily hard.

End of the Ceasefire

There comes a point in all wars when ceasefires come to an end and hostilities must recommence. At the beginning of March 2014, Emily came to us and told us she was now ready to recover. She was tired of stumbling through life, restricting everything she did, feeling so tired and weak, day in, day out. With anorexia, it's extremely challenging to stay put. You either get better or you get worse. You don't stay the same. In one of her more lucid periods, Emily came to the firm decision she wanted another crack at the Cardinal and recovery. Fortunately, we also had the benefit of a new year of BUPA funding and 45 days of in-patient stay were once again at our disposal.

Emily has acknowledged how ill she is and can see how distorted her thinking is. She would like the support of the clinic to recover from her anorexia. She does not feel that she can do this at home and said that it has gone on long enough and that she needs to get better. She recognises the consequences of remaining unwell and this really frightens her.

That was the opening paragraph in an email, dated 7th March, sent by one of the Cardinal Clinic's nurses to Emily and us. It outlined the contract drawn up between Emily and the Cardinal and it included a list of 20 dos and don'ts she had signed up to. This time around, there had to be real commitment shown by our daughter in advance that she was fully prepared to go with the plan. She had to demonstrate she was deadly serious about recovery.

But sadly, Ana didn't sign up to this.

Following discussion with Emily's parents, it has now been agreed that it would be appropriate for Emily to have an urgent referral to an NHS Inpatient Eating Disorder Unit. We have therefore discharged Emily from the Cardinal Clinic. Whilst Emily awaits admission, it would be appropriate for an urgent referral to the CMHT and CRISIS Team for assessment and support.

That was the letter written by the Cardinal Clinic to Emily's GP on 27th March 2014, just under three weeks after she had been admitted a second time around. The day before, Emily had cut her wrists and had been taken by ambulance in the middle of the night to Accident & Emergency. On her return to the Cardinal Clinic the following day, she had left the grounds and gone on a walkabout. She had ended up in a local garden centre. The pressure of having to gain weight was once again just too great. Emily was able to escape from the Cardinal easily enough, but she was finding it more difficult to escape from Ana's iron grip.

We were informed by the clinic that there was nothing else they could do for her. They were no longer able to guarantee her safety. The Cardinal was an open-style establishment with no locks on any doors. In their opinion, she would need an intensive 6-12-month stay in a secure eating disorder unit to have any chance of beating the illness.

In other words, we were going to need an even bigger boat.

FIXTURE LIST

- EARLY SKIRMISHES
  OCT 12 - APR 13 (W)/L

- BATTLE OF THE HIGHFIELD
  APR - JULY 13 (W)/L

- THE CEASEFIRE
  JULY - AUG 13 (W)/L

- THE CARDINAL CLINIC CRUSADES
  SEPT 13 - MAR 14 (W)/L

CHAPTER 16

THE COTSWOLD CAMPAIGN

(April to September 2014)

According to Chris Guillebeau, the American author, 'If plan A fails, remember there are 25 more letters.' At this rate, Mel and I were going to need all of them.[50]

It was the end of March 2014. Emily had failed to make any progress in the community on three separate occasions. In other words, recovery at home had not worked. She had also failed to make any progress at the Highfield Unit in Oxford over a three-month period or at the Cardinal Clinic in Windsor across two different stays, lasting another three months in total. Emily was now just over a month shy of her 18th birthday, at which point Mel and I would cease to have any legal jurisdiction over our daughter. Things were becoming desperate or, more accurately, we were becoming desperate.

Resilience has now become a popular term within the corporate environment and is seen as a "must-have attribute" for business professionals serious about climbing up the ladder. As a leader or manager, you will encounter plenty of obstacles, constraints, and setbacks and you need to do four things to demonstrate resilience: 1. Maintain your equilibrium; 2. Adjust to the ever-changing situation; 3. Hold on to some kind of control of the environment; 4. Keep moving forwards with a "can-do" mindset.

Or put more simply, resilience is 'the ability to become strong, healthy or successful again after something bad happens.'[51]

What both Mel and I found out was that it's surprisingly easy to be resilient when there is no other option. When your daughter is so very ill, and you seem to be her only hope, then resilient you must be. Like a boxer in a ring, we had been knocked down many times but each time the referee had been on the verge of stopping the fight, we got up, dusted off our gloves, and carried on with the battle. Our problem was that we just didn't know which round we were in and how many rounds were left to fight.

When Emily was last weighed at the Cardinal Clinic on 21st March 2014, the scales came in at 39.5kg (87 pounds). She was discharged from the clinic on 27th March. On 2nd April, she was assessed at Cotswold House, an NHS Specialist Eating Disorders

Unit in Oxford where the plan was to admit Emily as a long-term in-patient. She now weighed 37.4kg (82.5 pounds) and had dropped 2.1kg (4.7 pounds) in under two weeks. The reason for the dramatic drop was that her self-imposed meal plan included an apple for breakfast, a piece of toast at lunch and another piece of toast and a banana for dinner. She was drinking two to three glasses of water a day which wasn't enough.

To all intents and purposes, Emily had more or less stopped eating. She had given up on life. Ana had now abandoned her sister and was going in for the kill.

The big problem was there were no beds available at the Cotswold. There was a waiting list of a few weeks. When the consultant psychiatrist broke this news to our daughter, Emily told her she didn't know whether she could "survive for four weeks". She was crying out to be helped, because she was no longer able to help herself.

All the doctor could do was assure us her physical health would be monitored closely both by her GP and the CAMHS Crisis team. If Mel and I had any concerns about her wellbeing, we should take her to Accident & Emergency. If her condition was deemed to be life-threatening by the doctors there, she would be admitted. In other words, we had to wait until our daughter collapsed at home before we could do anything. That was one hell of a waiting game. It felt like we were playing Russian Roulette with her life.

Everybody was now in limbo, no one more so than Emily. At some point during the illness, she wrote a piece about how limbo feels. We have no recollection as to when she wrote it or where she was at the time, but it provides such an accurate narrative of her mental state during the worst of times that I thought I would share it here.

Limbo

I feel numb. Absolutely senseless. It's as if I am drifting through each day without purpose and without any idea of ~~where~~ where I'm going. My life no longer seems real; my reality is now a nightmare which I cannot wake up from. I am no longer a part of this world. I exist in Limbo.

Limbo is a place of nothingness. A place where nothing happens or matters. Imagine a black space with ~~no obje~~ objects, no lights and, most importantly, no gravity to keep you grounded – this is where I live, this is my limbo.

When people speak, the noise is muffled and unclear, yet the voices in my head are echoed and projected. My thoughts surround me, they fill my limbo with extreme noise from which I can't escape! When I'm alone, they get louder, so loud that I want to cover my ears and scream to block out the voices. They want me to suffer. Not just for a day or a week. They want me to suffer for a lifetime. In fact, they enjoy it. To see ~~my~~ me down and alone brings them happiness. Worst of all, they don't allow me to cry; tears are forbidden in limbo. Instead, they would rather see me wither away until I am nothing but an empty shell.

cont.

I feel like I am slowly but surely suff suffocating; every last feeling of happiness and love is ~~drained~~ drained away and replaced with sorrow and guilt. The never-ending guilt drives the sadness and the sadness feeds the voices - my world is like a vicious cycle which cannot be broken.

Limbo is merciless and cruel - there is simply no way out. There is nothing to hold on to. When you fall, you keep falling and falling.

Back to My Home Office

It was 3ʳᵈ April, the day after her assessment when we were told there were no beds. Time now for some resilience. I had to do something. It was up to me. I couldn't stay in limbo any longer.

So I sat down at my desk in our study at home and put my to-do list to one side. Work needed to be relegated to a slot later in the day. One thing I'd become much better at during this period was the ability to juggle plates. There was "Emily time", "work time", "Mel time", "Jack time", as well as a bit of "me-time". The last of these was not indulgent. It was essential for me to be able to keep my batteries charged. A walk with the dog, a pint or two in a pub with a friend, 30 minutes of bedtime reading. Mel had her own survival kit. We both had our own set of banisters.

I went on to my computer and looked up every single NHS eating disorders clinic in the UK. Over the course of the next two days, I phoned up each and every one of them. Nobody else was going to do it, so I did. I had nothing to lose. Unfortunately, each time I managed to get through to the right person, the response I got was depressingly consistent. 'We are very sorry to hear about your daughter, these must be very worrying times for you. However, we do not have any beds available at the moment. Good luck with your search.' Call after call, sympathetic rejection after sympathetic rejection.

Apparently, there was an eating disorder epidemic in the UK which meant there was a chronic shortage of beds. As we became more and more desperate, Mel and I briefly explored the possibility of going down the private route once again. But the money would have to come out of our own pockets. BUPA coverage would not have been sufficient. At £5,000 a week and with no guarantee of how long Emily would require as an in-patient, this just didn't seem to be a viable option. The Cardinal Clinic had suggested she would need long-term treatment, lasting as long as a year.

But if push had come to shove, we would have found the money somehow.

Eventually, we struck semi-lucky. A kind-hearted woman, Lynn St Louis, working at the Eating Disorders Service at the Bethlem Royal Hospital in South London, took one of my increasingly frantic calls. She heard my pleas sympathetically and explained a bed might be coming free within the next week or so. After calling our own GP, it was agreed the bed would be reserved for Emily. I was so relieved I could have cried. Interestingly, Lynn went on to tell me this was the first time she had ever had a father contacting them directly. It was always somebody from the NHS, a doctor or a member of staff from the CAMHS team, but never a desperate dad. I think I was a first.

On 9th April, a week after her first appointment, Emily's progress was reviewed at Cotswold House once again. Her weight was now 36.4kg (80 pounds). She had lost 1kg (2.2 pounds) in a week. There were still no beds available at the Cotswold. They promised they would also make contact with NHS England to see if a bed could be found out of area. Emily would continue to be monitored by the Crisis Team on a daily basis when her blood pressure and pulse would be checked.

She was hanging in there.

Back to the home study. Back to the list. "We are very sorry ...", "Unfortunately ...", "Good luck ..." The same old story. More resilience required.

They say that you can wait ages for a bus and then two suddenly come along at the same time. The following week, our luck changed for the better. During a 24-hour period, we had two bits of excellent news. Firstly, Lynn from the Bethlem Royal Hospital called to say a bed was now available and then Cotswold House got in touch to inform us one had also just come free in Oxford.

It honestly felt as if we had won the lottery. We were just so relieved. All of a sudden, we were spoilt for choice. I thanked Lynn profusely for all she had done, but we decided to take the offer of a bed at the Cotswold. This meant Emily would remain within the local system and our visits would involve the well-trodden 60-minute journey to Oxford rather than a two-hour slog across London.

Emily was admitted as an emergency to Cotswold House on Thursday 16th April 2014, 22 days after being discharged from the Cardinal Clinic. Her weight on admission was 34.9kg (77 pounds). She had lost just under 5kg (11 pounds) in just over three weeks. Her BMI was 13.8. In the report written by the consultant psychiatrist at the unit, this is how she assessed the risk:

Given Emily's poor dietary intake she is at high risk of physical decompensation, and without regular and careful re-feeding, she would be at high risk of mortality.

We had found a bed in the nick of time. Bad luck, Ana. Almost but not quite. We outsmarted you this time.

Cotswold House

Cotswold House was an eating disorders service for adults, provided by the Oxford Health NHS Foundation Trust. It first opened in 1994 and in addition to catering for both day- and outpatients, the facility also had 14 in-patient beds. Its main difference when compared to the Cardinal Clinic was it remained a specialist unit. It didn't deal with the wide range of mental health illnesses like alcohol or drug addiction but focused purely on eating disorders like anorexia and bulimia.[52]

When Emily was admitted, one bed was taken up by a male patient and all the others were occupied by females. There were all ages and backgrounds. As a parent, it was terrifying to see that anorexia didn't discriminate or give up. There were women in their early twenties, late twenties, and even one in her late forties. Once Ana had got her claws into you, she just wouldn't let go.

The other way in which it differed to the Cardinal was partly cosmetic. It didn't have either the trappings or trimmings of a private clinic, funded either by wealthy patients or the health insurance industry. There weren't any en-suite bathrooms, spacious living rooms where you could make yourself comfortable or well-manicured grounds to wander around during the day. Cotswold House was simple and functional by comparison, set up to get the job done, without the bells and whistles.

However, what both clinics did have in common was a team of skilled professionals who would give every ounce of their expertise and compassion to help the patients conquer their mental demons. It's just that the psychiatrists, psychologists, nutritionists, therapists, and carers at Cotswold House were able to focus single-mindedly on eating disorder demons.

They only dealt with monsters like Ana.

Nasogastric Intubation

During Emily's first couple of days at the Cotswold, she was put on what they called an 'A minus' diet. This was only 1,000kcal per day. For a healthy female of Emily's age, the average daily calorie intake is 2,000 to maintain weight and 2,500 if you want to increase your weight by 0.5kg (1 pound) per week. The reason why Emily couldn't jump straight from the 200 calories per day she was consuming before admission to the 2,500 calories level was that it would have been too much intake too quickly. Her internal systems could not have coped with so much food, so soon. The re-feeding process needed to be gradual and incremental.

The plan was to monitor her dietary intake very carefully, look out for any compensatory behaviours (in other words, watch out for Ana), and keep an eye on her physical parameters and bloods. If Emily was unable to complete her diet, a supplement would be given and if that failed, she would be offered Nasogastric Intubation, also known as NG feeding. This is where a doctor or nurse inserts a thin plastic tube through the nose of the patient, down the oesophagus and into the stomach. Once this tube is in place, they can use it to give you food and medicine. NG intubation is most commonly used for patients who have suffered back, neck or facial injuries, those who need a mechanical ventilator, or those who have an intestinal blockage or obstruction. In other words, this method of re-feeding is used for people who want to eat but who can't.

However, it is also used for people who need to eat but won't. After a couple of days at the clinic, Emily had a tube inserted into her nose and it remained there until she was out of the danger zone.

For the next few weeks, Emily's physical condition stabilised and her weight began to creep up, gram by gram. Two weeks after admission, it was 35.4kg (78 pounds). She had put on half a kilo (1 pound). Mentally, she also seemed a lot calmer, relieved she was being looked after once again. She felt she was in safe hands, a feeling shared by Mel and me. Although our daughter had reached rock bottom, we were convinced she was in the right place at last. She had a chance now, but it was still up to her whether to take it or not.

It remained her choice, as it always had been.

But things were still very tough for her. She was in the foot hills of Mount Everest and still had an awfully long way to go to reach the summit of recovery. Her carers gradually started putting pressure on her to eat more. You either go up or you go down. You don't stay put. Emily knew the drill. Mel and I were crossing all our fingers and all our toes. We knew only too well the acid test would come when Emily was presented with bigger plates of food in front of her. More calories to consume. That's when Ana would start shouting in her face, screaming in her ear, doing everything possible to derail our daughter.

Our first breakthrough

Emily turned 18 on 5th May 2014. That morning, at her bi-weekly weigh-in, she registered her first significant weight increase in the clinic. During the last four days, it had gone up by 0.4kg (1 pound). We went to a local pub on the outskirts of Oxford to celebrate (her birthday, rather than the weight increase). She was given special dispensation as it was her 18th and was allowed out for two hours between her clinic meals.

Emily was joined, as a surprise, by half a dozen of her closest school friends who had all stayed loyal to her throughout her illness. They didn't understand it any better than anybody else, but they didn't stop loving her, thinking of her, and praying she would get better. They just wanted the old Em back.

Although spending a couple of hours in a pub garden wasn't how either Emily or we would have wanted to celebrate her first significant birthday, I suppose at least Mel and I didn't have to worry about controlling a bunch of drunken, rampaging teenagers trashing the house.

The day Emily became an adult was the day we had our first big breakthrough. There was no magic medication. It wasn't something either the doctors or Mel or I had said. But just maybe, it was Emily's equivalent of a 10-ton truck.

The breakthrough was Emily herself. She had finally had enough. It might have been having tubes stuck up her nose or the sight of her best friends eating and drinking normally at the pub, talking about boyfriends or giggling about silly stuff. Or maybe it was getting to know the other in-patients in the clinic, all older than her, all of them urging our daughter to "get a move on" and recover quickly. They told her she didn't want to end up like them, still stuck with Ana in their mid-twenties, caught like flies in a spider's web. Whatever it was, Emily had become fed up with anorexia, and almost immediately, she made the conscious decision to just get on with it. It was time to get divorced from her evil twin sister, who, in spite of all her promises, hadn't done our daughter any favours during the last two years.

Enough was enough.

Over the next few weeks, she decided to engage with the programme and her weight started to increase as a result. During the next two months, her weight went up by almost 7kg (15 pounds). On the 14th July, it stood at 42kg (93 pounds). What was wonderful to observe was a steely determination in our daughter's attitude. Three months earlier, she seemed determined to kill herself. Now she seemed equally determined to kill off Ana.

And even though there were tears and minor tantrums along the way, she began climbing Everest. Emily was talking a language we had not heard for almost 18 months. Yes, she was still very nervous, and yes, eating food and putting on weight still terrified her but there was something in the tone of her texts that indicated a change in mood. There were lots of positive words and defiant exclamation marks. She was becoming less obsessed with herself and more thoughtful of those people around her who were doing their best to help her recover. Any mental illness brings out the selfish side in a person, so any sign of selflessness is always a good one.

The effect this change had on Mel and I was enormously positive too. Over the last 18 months, we had worked so hard to do our very best for our stricken daughter. Every decision we had taken, both big and small, right or wrong, had only been made in her best interests. And after every setback, we had learnt to recalibrate, readjust our expectations, and go again. We had been resilient, we had been decisive, and this was more remarkable for the fact that resilience and decisiveness were not generally two words that went hand in hand with Mark and Mel Simmonds. Well, certainly not Mark.

Our relationship with our daughter had now changed. Whenever we received encouraging texts from her, our hopes would always be lifted, and our replies would be immediate and effusive. Even if I was away on business in a different time zone, I would find time to respond as quickly as possible and would always press "send" with a smile on my lips. Finally, we were beginning to behave like role model Dolphins and St Bernards. We were patient, understanding, and loyal, and we were finding it a whole lot easier to adopt a language that encouraged, coaxed, and guided. For the time being, there were no Rhinos, Terriers, Ostriches or Jellyfish in sight because we were getting such positive signals from Emily. We were now working together as a single team, all sharing the same single-minded objective.

Get rid of Ana once and for all.

Even the devil herself seemed to be more subdued. Maybe she felt she had now met her match. Being stuck in solitary confinement in the Cardinal for a couple of weeks was one thing. Being interned in the Cotswold for what looked like it was going to be a very long time, surrounded by a specialist team of "Ana beaters" was quite another. This was no fun at all. Even the other Anas in the ward seemed a lot more sensible, a lot more mature.

Suddenly, we saw glimpses of the promised land and we wanted to play our part in helping Emily get there. And despite the fact that others around her were not finding the recovery process very easy or straightforward, Emily just put her head down, stayed "in the zone", continued eating and putting on weight. We were so proud of her. After nearly two dire years of suffering bad news and disappointment, we seemed to be turning the corner.

Some Respite

Emily had been in the Cotswold for about four months. Mel and I had got into a steady routine, and once our daughter started to turn things around on her 18th birthday party, we began to relax a little.

From a work point of view, I was still getting a good amount of work from Brand Learning. Again, this was a huge relief. I was also beginning to travel abroad a bit more, with the quiet confidence that I wasn't going to get any "please call me as soon as you can" texts from Mel or any distant cries of help from Emily. Creative Creatures was still sleeping fairly soundly underground, although there were some encouraging murmurings from time to time when small projects popped up every now and then.

During this period, both Mel and I were able to enjoy a bit more "us-time". We got the respite we desperately needed. We took it in turns to spend some time away from the front line as the Cotswold squadron continued the engagement with Ana. Mel went on a short, much-deserved mini-break to Mallorca with her girlfriends to celebrate her 50th and I managed to get away with my two sons on a "lads and dad" week in Crete. It was great to reconnect properly with both Will and Jack for a few days, enjoy some banter as well as some beers together. But it certainly wasn't "business as usual" on any front. How could it be when your daughter was locked away in an eating disorder clinic? I had some interesting conversations on holiday when I tried to explain to fellow tourists the reason why I was on holiday with my two boys, unaccompanied by my wife and daughter.

But relative to what we had experienced during the last couple of years, these were better times. They felt more normal.

How and Why Not to Stop Halfway

Emily had now spent 18 weeks in the clinic and on 18th August, her weight reached 45kg (99 pounds) for the first time in over a year and a half. Her BMI was just under 18, within touching distance of 18.5, the healthy minimum. At the Cotswold, they had two separate eating areas. One was for the people who were still really struggling. The other was for those who had overcome the worst of their eating disorder and were beginning to have a much healthier relationship both with their food and with their bodies. They needed less supervision. That's where Emily found herself now. The different therapies available were beginning to have some impact because her brain was now sufficiently nourished to absorb what was being said. It was no longer a barrel with a hole in it.

The talk in the clinic was now not if she could be discharged but when.

Emily's self-imposed target had been to leave the Cotswold when her BMI reached 19. In fact, she left when it was just above the 18 mark.

In hindsight, this was a big mistake.

Partial recovery is a common outcome in anorexia. Just because you reach the minimum healthy weight, it doesn't mean your eating disorder suddenly stops. You don't just look at a plate of chips and think to yourself, 'I'm fine now. I'll have that!' In order to have any chance of conquering the illness, common medical wisdom suggests you have to overshoot the 19 mark by quite a margin. You have starved your body for God knows how long, so the last thing it wants now is to feel like it is still being rationed. In layman's terms, it needs to gorge itself on the food and drink it has been deprived of before it then says, 'Okay, I'm good now.' Your body will tell you when you have reached the right weight and not the other way around.

Emily had spent so long trying to get to a healthy BMI and she was now really close to it. Everybody kept mentioning that magic number, 18.5. This had been her target, her goal, and she was simply a few grams short. No big deal. She had spent five months inside a clinic surrounded by other patients, many of whom were far more ill than her. Some of them would never recover from their eating disorder. Emily believed she had recovered enough and now wanted "out". She had kicked Ana into the long grass and she was impatient to restart her life once again. She needed to make up for lost time and already had big plans in place. She was going to take her driving test, go travelling to Australia and New Zealand, possibly try to get back into full-time education.

Mel and I wanted Emily to stay in the clinic a bit longer and put on another kilo or two (two to four pounds) to give herself some buffer. She was adamant, however, that being surrounded by very ill patients all the time was no longer helping her recovery.

Emily could be very persistent, bordering on stubborn. She was now. In any case, she was 18 and so the decision to leave or to stay was hers to make with the doctors.

She was discharged from Cotswold House as an in-patient on the 4th September.

We were so proud of what our daughter had achieved during her time in Oxford. She had been at death's door and had pulled herself back from the brink. It had been an almighty struggle, but she had succeeded. It was her victory. And although she hadn't quite reached the top of Mount Everest, she was now on a ledge only 200 feet short.

Unfortunately, you can't stop just 200 feet short of the summit. It's precarious and the weather is extremely inhospitable. It's impossible to stay there for long. You only have two options. You either find the strength to climb to the very top or you descend to the very bottom, voluntarily or involuntarily, quickly or slowly. Anorexia is no different. Emily was going to discover how tricky it was to try to stay just beneath the summit.

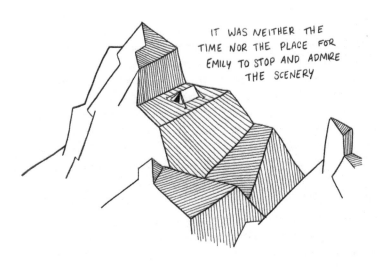

IT WAS NEITHER THE TIME NOR THE PLACE FOR EMILY TO STOP AND ADMIRE THE SCENERY

CHAPTER 17

WE ARE ASSETS NOT LIABILITIES

Miss Simmonds worked very hard on the ward to restore her weight. She took a mature approach in order to avoid premature discharge and the possibility of relapse, despite feeling much better. She reached a stage where she was no longer putting on weight but was psychologically more at ease with the idea of eating and weight gain. She was given increasing periods of leave from the ward which had been successful, before transferring her to day patient care. She continued attending Cotswold House as a day patient and was discharged back to the Buckinghamshire service on 24/9/14.

This was the glowing end-of-term report Emily had received. Unfortunately, this positive outcome was not always the case with patients at Cotswold House. That was the evil nature of anorexia nervosa, an illness which would chalk up more victories than it would sustain losses. Mel and I were so relieved. Even though nobody was quite sure what the future held for our daughter, including Emily herself, we had got her back in one piece. Ana had failed in her mission. We had won, Ana had lost. My Winner gene had something to cheer about at long last and my Worry gene could relax for a bit.

As soon as Emily left the Cotswold, she took charge of her life once again. She had been given clear guidance by the clinic on what to do and what not to do as far as her eating routines were concerned. She was a vegetarian and eating healthily was her number one priority "on the outside". She now had her own set of banisters to hold on to when her staircase became rickety. She was much healthier, looked more like any other normal teenager, and seemed so much more content in herself. Everybody around her was smiling too.

Crazy Maisie

After just a couple of weeks of freedom, a very well-meaning friend decided to give Emily a present to help aid her recovery. A kitten, called Maisie. Mel's and my initial reaction was mixed. A lovely gesture for sure, but ... Well, put it this way, we knew who would be looking after her. But we kept Maisie and we soon fell in love with her, partly because she was damaged. She had inherited a neurological disorder at birth which meant she "wobbled" when she walked. It also meant she was skittish and easily frightened. But she was also very affectionate. They often say dogs are like their owners. Purdey was very loyal and forgiving. She was always unperturbed and nonplussed by events unfolding around her. Mel was like Purdey. I don't think they say cats are like their owners, but if so, I think Maisie was more like me.

When it comes to marriage, conventional wisdom states that opposites often attract. Mel developed a real soft spot for Maisie, partly because she was coping with life, despite being somewhat limited by her condition.

Maybe that's why Mel was so attracted to me?

Emily's Gap Year

Emily was now fiercely determined to make up for lost time. She learnt to drive and passed her test quickly. She loved the new-found freedom she had acquired both from Cotswold House and, through the car, from us at home. In theory, Emily was now on her gap year, albeit a slightly unconventional one. Instead of A Levels it had been two years of anorexia, and instead of university ... Well, at that point, we weren't very sure what it would be. We were in uncharted waters. However, Emily was going to do all the things "normal" gap year students do, and that included travelling. So, during November and December, she went to Australia and New Zealand. She accompanied me on a flight to Sydney where I was running a week-long workshop and spent some time with my brother who lived out there with his family. They could keep a watchful eye on her. She then went touring on her own for six weeks, returning just before Christmas.

Eight months earlier she was confined to an NHS bed in Oxford with a tube stuck up her nose. Now she was snorkelling among the marine life on the Great Barrier Reef.

In January 2015, she received two pieces of welcome news.

First of all, having undergone a rigorous audition before going to Australia, she succeeded in getting a job at Disneyland Paris, working as a character performer and parade entertainer. Think Winnie the Pooh, Fauna the Fairy, Mickey Mouse, Chip and Dale, and that was our Emily. Secondly, she managed to secure a place at Durham University on a full-time Foundation course, starting in the autumn. This was a one-year programme, designed for people like her who had missed out on their A Levels for a particular reason, for mature adults who wanted a second crack at education later in their lives or for foreign students who want to study in Britain. Once you passed this course, you had the opportunity to enrol on a full-time degree.

Based to a large extent on an excellent set of GCSE exam results when she was 16, Emily had won a place at one of the top universities in the UK. As parents, we were simply overjoyed. Despite everything that had happened during the previous two and a half years, somehow or other, our daughter seemed to be back in the mainstream.

Rightly or wrongly, Mel and I were secretly relieved that the conversations we could now have with our friends had changed from the Cardinal Clinic and the Cotswold House to Disneyland and Durham. Happy days!

Emily spent five months in Paris, entertaining wide-eyed children from all over the world, living independently, and earning money. She was secure in the knowledge that she had her place at university in the autumn. She had ended up enjoying a proper gap year. Imagine how relieved she must have been now having different kinds of conversations with her own friendship set. And just imagine how relieved they must have been too.

During August of that year, we went on a two-week holiday to Corfu, the first family holiday for three years. And in October, Emily went off to Durham where she completed her Foundation course in Arts and Humanities, achieving a "First" for the year with an overall average of 73%. It was the summer of 2016. Happy, happy days.

Functioning Anorexic

Here's what really happened between September 2014 and June 2016.

Our daughter did emerge from Cotswold House with that glowing report, but she wasn't in charge of her life completely. Ana was still hanging around, still hassling, still whispering, still cajoling.

Post-discharge, her weight hovered around the 45kg (99 pounds) mark with a BMI of around 18 (still not the minimum healthy target). Emily did everything possible to maintain weight without necessarily wanting to increase it, and so she ate accordingly. Her mental calorie counter made sure she knew exactly what was going into her body. She had just about accepted the look and feel of her own body shape as it was. At this moment in time, further weight increase was definitely not on her agenda.

When she went to Australia and New Zealand, she stuck to foods and restaurants where she knew precisely what she was eating and how much. She wouldn't consider the food if calories weren't clearly indicated on the pack or the menu, Alcohol was strictly off limits. She came back from her trip, sun-tanned but skeletal. She had lost 5kg (11 pounds) and was now down to 40kg (88 pounds) once again. Christmas wasn't a lot of fun that year either.

Calories, always calories.

In the new year, and after a bit of painful soul-searching, she found the willpower to put herself on an intensive weight-increase diet for a month, regained the pounds she had lost down under. But once again, she stopped at 45kg (99 pounds), 200 feet short of the summit.

We had always been told the last 200 feet were the hardest.

In Disneyland Paris, it was more of the same. Extremely controlled eating, doing everything possible to maintain her weight but not to increase it. After three or four months in Paris, an over exuberant Spanish boy tugged at her Remy the Rat's costume nose and she sustained a relatively serious neck injury. She was forced to rest and recover for a few weeks. She stayed in Paris, but not only did she stop working, she also stopped eating properly. The exercise the active job had provided up until that point was the counter-balance to the food she was consuming. No exercise, no food. That was the deal she had struck with herself. That was her self-imposed balancing act.

As a result, the weight dropped, dropped, and dropped again. Finally, she broke down and returned home in July in somewhat of a mess, physically and emotionally.

We had already booked our family holiday to Corfu. After plenty of discussion and deliberation, we decided to go ahead with it, but the only way this would be possible was if Emily could bring out her own suitcase of essential foods. This might at least ensure she maintained her weight. So, at every meal we had either in the villa or in a local taverna, Emily would pull out her plastic Tupperware container with a healthy humus pot, a few crackers, a yoghurt and a Diet Coke inside. The rest of us would tuck in to our Greek salads, Moussaka, and wine aplenty.

When we got back home at the end of August, the question was whether Emily was well enough to go to Durham in October. The three of us decided another in-patient stay at the Cardinal might just do the trick. We had BUPA funding available. Although the clinic hadn't worked out on her two previous visits, Emily wanted to make it succeed this time around. She understood how the Cardinal set-up worked, she liked and respected the staff there. And she knew if she could put on a few kilograms and get used to eating proper food, then she might have a fighting chance of surviving halls of residence and university life. Relatively speaking, she was in a much better place now than she had been in her two previous stays at the Cardinal. She realised this would be her only realistic chance to get the weight boost she needed to get to Durham. She probably realised too that this was her only chance of escaping her nagging parents and a limited life in Stewkley.

As parents, we were also extremely eager not to lose what we saw as a terrific opportunity for Emily to get back on track. Desperate measures for desperate times.

It was touch and go, but Emily made good enough progress in the clinic during her three-week stay. She put on a few kilos and ate better, far better than she had done in Corfu a few weeks earlier. At the clinic, she just had no choice but to eat.

After much deliberation, Emily finally decided she wanted to give Durham a crack. It had proved to be the burning platform she needed.

Mel and I were relieved.

She did survive the academic year at Durham and somehow managed to pass with flying colours. But it was extremely hard for her and it was hard for us as parents too. She never ate in the refectory, always alone in her own room, where she could control what she consumed. She rarely went out to any restaurants, never drank any alcohol, and, as a result, her social life was severely restricted by her self-imposed constraints. This put a great strain on her as well as her newly acquired friends, who had not really bargained on propping up an anorexic in their first year at university. Unsurprisingly, they just wanted to have fun. If it had been three or four years earlier, Emily would have wanted the same. The Durham experience also continued to put enormous pressure on Mel and me. We were on call 24 / 7 to provide long-distance support and counselling conversations, and had to embark on very long road trips up north, every now and then.

When she finished her course in June 2016, she decided not to progress to the full-time degree. She couldn't see herself studying academic theory for a further three years and it was also just becoming too difficult for her to manage life at university, physically, socially, or emotionally.

Emily was still ill. She still had anorexia. The common term for people like Emily in her semi-recovered condition is a "functioning anorexic". Somebody who restricts what they eat and drink so they can maintain a weight with which they are comfortable, but one which is often unhealthy. In other words, a BMI of less than 18.5. Unfortunately, the negative impact of this restriction makes it nigh on impossible to complete challenges or activities that require high degrees of effort, endurance, or concentration. If she had been happy living at home, holding down a local part-time bar job, never having kids, then she could remain a functioning anorexic. But Emily wanted to travel the world, accomplish great things, work hard, and play hard. But she couldn't. It simply wasn't possible. She had to make a choice. If she wanted to live locally for the rest of her life, then she could stay as she was. If she wanted to go for the moon, then she had to recover fully.

During the summer after she finished at Durham, it felt as if we were back to square one. We were now in year four of the Anorexia Wars and Mel and I felt so frustrated. We still remembered so clearly just how much Emily had going for her before she became ill. A lovely, bubbly personality, with so much innate ability. And even during the period of her illness, she had accomplished so much. She had written tear-jerkingly moving poems, created wonderfully expressive paintings, cared deeply for other fellow strugglers, visited the southern hemisphere, lived and worked in Paris, studied at Durham University ... And she had done all of this with Ana hanging around her neck.

She was like a professional athlete who breaks their ankle badly but who remains competitive even though they are still on crutches. Just imagine how good they would be if they had allowed their injury to heal properly, if they were completely fit. The same was true with Emily. She had so many assets just waiting to be fully unleashed. But she couldn't completely let go of Ana and that's what was holding her back from competing fully in the game of life.

She was hobbling along and we were hobbling along behind her. It was painful for all of us.

Still in the Trenches

During the period between 2013 and 2015 my workload had remained high. My colleagues at both Imparta and Brand Learning, where I was still freelancing, were aware of my tricky situation at home. They remained very supportive and kept pushing work my way. This meant I didn't have to worry about paying the bills at least. That had been a huge relief. One less thing to fret over.

However, at the beginning of 2016, my freelance work came to a grinding halt for different reasons. In fact, January of that year was the first one in my career as an independent when I earned nothing at all. Not a dime. I had been caught napping. There is always the risk when working as a freelancer that there will be peaks and troughs, so my initial reaction was just that. This is just another trough. The next peak will be just around the corner. Frustratingly, this trough remained a trough for month after month, and suddenly we had money worries to add to our Emily worries.

Although her condition was not acute, and her weight was still hovering just below the healthy BMI mark, she remained a functioning anorexic, still focusing on surviving more than living. Mel and I remained unsure whether the war with Ana would ever end. Every now and then, another mortar shell would explode nearby and we would run for cover.

Plan (I Lose Count of Which Letter)

Emily was now 19. Since leaving Durham in June, she had taken some time off to consider her long-term options before she began to embark on another little adventure.

This was a somewhat unusual one. It was also typical Emily.

She had always loved sport and being outside, and she was equally passionate about the performing arts, dance, and drama in particular. Disneyland Paris had given her a taste of all of these. By putting them together, a career opportunity had now become blindingly obvious to her. Wait for it ... She would train to become a professional stunt performer!

Although Mel and I were slightly incredulous at first, this idea did have some substance as well as some merit. Knowing Emily before she got ill, this kind of thing would have suited her down to the ground. The qualification involved becoming proficient in six different disciplines, some fairly extreme. Emily chose gymnastics, judo, swimming, high diving, rock climbing, and scuba diving from the accredited list. Once you reached the required standards in each, you were placed on the official Stunt Register and this gave you license to work on film sets across the world. Even though we remained highly sceptical, we went along with Emily's plan, partly because there was potentially a hidden benefit. The training regime she signed up for across the disciplines was physically very demanding. This meant she would have to view her body in a new light. Less like an aesthetic object of beauty, more like a functional instrument that could help her reach her goals.

In other words, the side benefit was she would have to put on weight to become stronger. Could stunt performing be the Trojan Horse that would guide her back to fitness, health, and wellbeing?

No, it couldn't.

Unfortunately, Emily did everything she could to defy the laws of body biomechanics. She tried her hardest to maintain her weight at 45kg and cope with the rigorous training involved at the same time. She struggled to make the standards required in her chosen disciplines because she wasn't physically strong enough.

She was becoming increasingly frustrated and despondent, and that was usually the time that Ana pounced.

We Are Assets Not Liabilities

In February 2017, Emily got a lucky break. During the previous summer, she had got down to the last four applicants in a very competitive field to become an apprentice at ITV. She didn't quite make it, but a few months later she was offered the opportunity to work as a runner at ITV's The London Studios, where all kinds of shows like *Loose Women*, *Good Morning Britain*, and *The Graham Norton Show* were filmed. The runner role was the bottom rung of the career path in television, but it was a proper job.

Both Mel and I were apprehensive that Emily was not robust enough, either mentally or emotionally, to hold down a job in London. Her eating was still very disordered. But we felt this was a chance worth taking. If she could embrace London life, discover some self-esteem in the corporate world, and find some new friends, maybe it would be sufficient incentive to replace Ana.

So, we started nudging Emily back into the mainstream. It was time for her ship to head out for the open seas and leave the relative safety of the harbour in Stewkley. Still close enough for us to keep a watchful eye over her, but far enough away for her to get the independence she craved. Unfortunately, she was also joining the legion of people who desperately try to lead a typical existence while not really being typical at all. Individuals who suffered with mental health disorders but kept that side of themselves hidden from the public eye. That was the risk we were taking when we took Emily to the flat share in Clapham Common to meet her new housemates and start the next chapter of her life.

Unfortunately, Ana was still lurking in the vicinity.

During the next few weeks, Emily got stuck in to her job and into London life. She always gave everything her very best shot. That was her nature. But she couldn't bring herself to let anybody know, either her new work colleagues or her new housemates, that she was still struggling. More than anything, after five years of being different to everyone else, she wanted to at least pretend to the outside world she was now the same as them.

She'd do everything possible to hide her condition and camouflage her gremlins. She would make excuses as to why she couldn't go out and eat in the evenings, bring carefully prepared packed lunches in to work, and remain suitably vague and elusive about her traumatic past. Emily's Winner gene had helped her land a great opportunity to get her back on track, but the same gene was now insisting that her grim past remain hidden from the public eye.

From my experiences, I knew this was a dangerous path to follow. When I returned to work in November 2001, I found it relatively easy to be open about my problems with mental health, possibly because my experience had been so dramatic and so public. I found that owning up and being honest helped to release the pressure valve in my brain. It also ensured I could manage a return to work on my own terms. I was never ashamed of my illness, but maybe that's the understandable difference between a 39-year-old with a few years under his belt and a 21-year-old just venturing out into adult life. We encouraged Emily to open up and own up, but she remained highly reluctant to do so.

After two months at ITV, the combination of long hours, a physically demanding and stressful job, and the pressure of concealing the truth from all those around her became unbearable. Emily suffered a breakdown at work. As her weight began to plummet once more, her body became physically exhausted and her fragile mind could no longer cope.

The game was up, and it was now time for her to come clean.

Fortunately for Emily, her boss, Susie, although taken aback by the unfolding events, was hugely supportive. She ordered my daughter to take two weeks off immediately and kept in constant contact with her over this period. When Emily returned to work, she took some time to explain her painful past to Susie. Her boss remained nonplussed, unfazed. She promised to keep a watchful eye, and contracted with her that if she was feeling in any way "wobbly" over the next few weeks, she should come in to her office and talk things through.

The Dolphin / St Bernard hybrid approach was just what was now needed.

However, what remains the most impressive aspect of Susie's positive attitude towards my daughter was that she didn't lose faith in her ability or potential as a professional. In fact, from that point on, Susie helped Emily push forward with her career at ITV by encouraging her to express her talents, giving her the confidence she needed to start moving up from the bottom rung of the corporate ladder. But she always remained vigilant, mindful of where Emily was mentally and where she had come from.

What Susie demonstrated was that it's important not to see mental health sufferers as "damaged property" but to treat them as people with an illness that might rear its ugly head every now and then. Ironically, they could also be viewed as untapped sources of potential. If Emily had fought so hard to get where she was despite what she had been through, how good might she become if she could be coaxed gently towards some kind of full recovery?

It became obvious to me that the immediate boss of somebody suffering from mental illness would always play a critical role in determining whether that person flourished or floundered, whether they reached their full potential or sank into obscurity.

I came across another inspiring example of this boss / subordinate relationship being played out.

This one was slightly higher profile.

Alastair Campbell and Tony Blair

Alastair Campbell suffered a breakdown in the mid-1980s. When Tony Blair became leader of the Labour Party in 1994, he asked Campbell to work with him, but the latter was unsure whether to accept or not. Conscious of the pressure he was likely to be under in the new role and very mindful of his past experiences with both depression and breakdowns, Campbell asked if he could take a month to think about the offer. Blair then took the bull by the horns, came down to France where his friend was on holiday and tried to persuade him to accept the role.

On a car journey back from Marseilles airport, Campbell decided to come completely clean.

'And so, I'm driving and I'm talking away about all the stuff that happened in my head and the drink and the psychosis and the hospitalisation and getting arrested and all this sort of stuff. And I can see him going "This is all a bit weird ..." And anyway, so we'd yatter away like this and then eventually he said, "Well look I'm not bothered if you're not bothered." And I said, "Yes but what if I'm bothered?" He said, "Well I'm still not bothered".'

According to Campbell, Blair fully grasped what had happened to his friend and the painful experiences he had gone through. He was able to empathise with how he was thinking and feeling. However, he was able to make a "bigger, deeper, broader judgement". Ultimately, Blair showed great faith in Campbell. He didn't think that there would be a problem and after that there never really was.[53]

Walk the Walk and Talk the Talk

Individuals who have suffered from mental health disorders, minor or major, should be treated as valuable assets rather than weak liabilities. The experiences they have gained, the pain they have suffered, the deep insights they have developed both about themselves and others should be seen as a rich, creative resource to be used by society at large.

It is vital that senior leaders in the corporate world take off their blinkers, understand mental illness for what it is and work their absolute hardest to maximise the potential of those people who are suffering currently or who have suffered in the past. Their actions will always speak louder than their words alone. Susie did that for Emily and I know that she will be forever grateful. Tony Blair did it for Alastair Campbell and I am sure he is too.

Our daughter was back working at ITV in London. Mel and I breathed another deep sigh of relief. Crisis averted. For now.

We were slowly approaching the fifth anniversary of our daughter's unforgiving illness. We were starting to hope we might just be winning the war and that some kind of "full recovery" was within touching distance. We also knew that as far as Emily was concerned, continuing to live life as a functioning anorexic was incompatible with achieving total contentment or satisfaction, either personally or professionally.

We now believed Emily realised this too. At long last. But the choice was still hers to make. Not ours.

She had that same 200 feet to climb.

TIME FOR THE
FINAL ASCENT?

CHAPTER 18

BACK-TO-BACK TESTS

Viktor Emil Frankl was an Austrian neurologist and psychiatrist. He was also a Holocaust survivor who lived to ninety-two. He devoted most of his life to understanding, studying and promoting the meaning of "meaning". The book for which he is most famous, *Man's Search for Meaning*, provides a graphic account of how he managed to survive the horrors of the Holocaust by finding a positive way of relating to his experiences. What he noticed was that it was the prisoners who were prepared to comfort others in greater need, the ones who gave away their last morsel of stale bread, who survived the longest. On the other hand, those who allowed the camp surroundings to eat away at and destroy their inner belief systems were the ones who fell victim fastest. Frankl summed things up perfectly: "If there is meaning in life at all, then there must be meaning in suffering".[54]

Mel and I were no Viktor Frankl. Not by a long, long way. But we knew what he meant about giving meaning to suffering. We had all certainly suffered through Emily's illness, no one more so than Emily herself. But if we ended up guiding her to a better place, then that was all that mattered.

As the expression goes, "what doesn't kill you, makes you stronger."

Caring for somebody in the depths of a challenging illness does have some silver linings. The focus of your attention must remain outwards rather than inwards. You become proactive rather than reactive. Somebody else desperately needs your help and you have to step up to the plate, because nobody else will. This sense of clear purpose gives you strength and direction. You aren't frightened of making big decisions because there's no option but to make them.

I didn't know it at the time, but I was about to be challenged over the next 18 months in two quite different ways. Life would set me a couple of tests to see how much I had learnt since 2001. It wanted to judge whether I had made any progress and how strong the banisters really were.

The Dakar Rally was about to get interesting.

First Test – the Final 200 Feet

In July 2017, when Emily had returned to work at ITV after her mini breakdown, it had been touch and go whether she would come back to London or not. There had been pros and cons.

Cons first. She was obviously not able to cope with an intensive job in London when she was still in the shackles of Ana. There was scant evidence she possessed the willpower to change her status from "functioning anorexic" to "recovered anorexic". Her job as a runner was just as the title implies. She ran all over the place for 10 hours every day. Escorting guests and celebrities to and from shows, hunting down props across the city, carrying out errands here, there, and everywhere. Ana must have been licking her lips, watching her burning up all those calories.

Surely it was better now to put up our hands, admit defeat once again, keep Emily at home and do all we could to help her regain weight in the safety of Stewkley.

Many of our friends thought this was the only sensible solution.

Pros next. Emily had only been in London for a few months, and we hadn't really given things a proper go. Her weight hadn't dropped significantly and, although her eating was still disordered, there had been some progress with her routines. She had started seeing an excellent London nutritionist who understood where she was at and was keen to help her recover. We had also tried the "let's get Emily better at home" treatment regime several times before and it had never succeeded. Why should it work now? Neither Mel nor I had developed any further powers of persuasion and the environment would be depressingly familiar to Emily. We also felt that coming back home would be a blow to her self-esteem, involving more difficult explanations to her friends who were all moving on with their lives.

This felt like the last chance saloon for Emily. Did she really want to settle for the life of a functioning anorexic with all its inherent limitations? Would life in a small, rural English village represent the full scope of her ambition? Mel and I were now beginning to prepare ourselves for this eventuality. We had run out of plans, there were no more letters of the alphabet left.

This was plan Z.

Fortunately for all concerned, Emily didn't want to be left behind. Her short taste of a different life, a far more fulfilling one, was sufficient enough to give her the courage to try London one last time. Even though she wasn't sure she would be able to cope, she decided to give it a go. Mel and I backed her decision to return to the capital. Intuitively, we felt this was the right thing to do, borne out of gut feel rather than any hard proof.

So we gently pushed her back out to sea again, wearing a life jacket, and we remained in the lifeboat not far behind. We were always within spitting distance.

Our greatest test throughout the next few months would be to try to emulate proper Dolphins. We had failed miserably during the height of Emily's anorexia when we were all under so much pressure. Rhinos and Terriers were always our animals of choice. Emily was now 21 years old and required a different parental approach. She was an adult and had to start taking ownership for her own actions, and our role was to coach rather than coerce, mentor rather than micromanage.

However, we did make one strong suggestion as she prepared to head south again. We urged her to bare her soul, explain her traumatic past both to her work colleagues and to her housemates. She had to attempt something different to break the mould. We strongly felt this could help release the pressure.

After some initial hesitation, she heeded our advice. It worked wonders. Everybody was very supportive, so impressed she had decided to come clean. The weight came off her tired shoulders. With the ongoing support of her boss, Susie, and others around her who were now "in the know", she walked around town with a spring in her step and a smile on her face.

She had climbed the first 50 feet. Another 150 to go.

Benny

Emily also received help from a totally unexpected source.

David Bennett (Benny) was an old university friend. I hadn't seen him for about 10 years when he called me up out of the blue and said he was going to be in the Oxford area. How about if he came to stay? Perfect. Except that the day he came to visit was the day Emily had broken down at work. She would come back home later that day to stay for a couple of weeks.

Benny and I went to the pub that Friday evening and he told me what he was up to. His occupation wasn't so very different to mine. He was a coach in both the business and personal arenas and had just started practising a new kind of coaching based on The Three Principles / Inside-Out understanding.[55]

Being somewhat of a theory nut, I was intrigued. Benny explained some of the underlying philosophy. For example, what we feel is 100% correlated to our thinking in the moment. So when we are feeling well, we will often be experiencing a flow of healthy thinking. But a virus, like Ana, can creep into the system and begin transmitting unhealthy messages through thought, which, if paid attention to, can lead to unhealthy emotions and behaviours.

But however much we might have lost our way, there is always a place inside us that remains intact, healthy, and whole. Our true self, if you like. Healthy messages continue to be sent from that place, guiding us back on track even if they are temporarily drowned out by a powerful intruder like Ana.

The key for Emily, as Benny saw it, was to remember that she always had this magical place inside her. She could then start to listen out for the healthy messages it was transmitting and pay less attention to the unhealthy ones Ana kept on sending her, allowing for more and more access to her true self would eventually lead to a natural self-correction.

Much easier said than done, I know, but I applauded the simplicity of the approach.

It seemed very intuitive.

Benny then took the bull by the horns and offered to help Emily there and then, the very day she got home, slightly traumatised by her breakdown at work. I resisted his kind offer. Emily was too fragile to absorb anything new. She was still in a state of shock. Over the next 24 hours, Benny gently persisted. Could he just have two minutes with Emily before he went? That's all he wanted. I agreed to his request.

He said just two things to her. Firstly, using this approach, he had helped a girl like Emily when she was also suffering from anorexia. Secondly, there was no homework involved; no sitting down twice a day for 20 minutes to meditate; no having to keep a daily diary of your thoughts and feelings. That was it, he was done. He said his goodbyes and left.

Three days later, Emily, still on sick leave, came to me and asked if she could talk to Benny. She had reflected on what she had heard during those two minutes, and it had resonated with her. We arranged for a Skype call the next weekend, and from that point on, for the next six months, Emily enjoyed one of the very few productive coaching relationships she'd had with anybody during the five years of her illness.

That October, Emily went on holiday to Marrakech for a short mini-break with Mel, her first holiday for two and a half years. And for the first time in five years, she started to enjoy her food. She tried new dishes she had never had before, explored new tastes, new flavours. There was no calorie counting, no weighing of the food. She just ate and drank. Normally.

Mel was both dumbstruck and delighted. Had Emily finally turned the corner? Was this the moment we had been waiting for, praying for? Neither Mel nor I were popping the champagne corks just yet. We had been stung too many times before to even think about celebrating. But there was hope. Definitely some hope.

100 feet to go.

Benny played a key role in Emily's revival, but the combination of several people and many things also helped her turn the corner. It was the realisation that being in London, working in a job and for a company many people her age would kill for, was too good an opportunity to waste. With every passing week, she was getting more and more plaudits from her colleagues. They loved her hard work ethic, all the more so as they now knew the dark place from which she had just emerged.

There was nothing left for her at home in Stewkley, except two war-scarred parents beating the same old drum. And part-time jobs in pubs and restaurants didn't provide her with any great incentive to return home.

Maybe she was also tired of Ana who had promised so much over the years and yet delivered so little. Emily was becoming happier and healthier and it had nothing to do with her surrogate sister. She wasn't the great friend she had pretended to be all along. She was a fraud.

No, it wasn't Benny alone, but without a shadow of a doubt, his patient style of coaching and his fresh approach certainly helped Emily enormously, when it was needed most. She would contact him on an "as-needed" basis and he would always "play what was in front of him". Never prescriptive, always going with Emily's flow and energy. He became a coach, sounding board, refresher course, all rolled up into one.

Thanks, Benny.

50 feet to go.

The detailed report Mel and I jointly received from Life after this first test was very encouraging. The comment that pleased us both was as follows: "You have both begun to demonstrate excellent Dolphin behaviours with regard to your daughter. This is encouraging her to find her own way in life. You are providing her with the right amount of guidance and support. Very well done!" However, this was quickly followed by a word of warning. "Things are still likely to be up and down over the next few months and there will be hiccups along the way. Make sure you keep your Rhino and Terrier tendencies in check when the pressure is on. Mel, in particular." (My Winner gene found it hard to suppress a smug little smile.)

Second Test – the Financial Crisis of 2016 / 2017

On the business front, the commercial situation remained precarious. In 2016, my freelance work dried up completely. I had to take action fast if we were going to stay afloat financially. I was now 54 years old and had a stark choice to make. I could either try to establish new relationships with other marketing capability agencies, secure some regular income. This was fundamentally playing things safe. Or could I become a little bit more adventurous and find more imaginative ways of earning some income? I never had any intention of taking any "silly risks" which would only expose me to further pressure I didn't need. But was there a "safe risk" option, one that could play to my strengths, while keeping me well clear of deep and dangerous waters?

The answer was obvious. How about if I went back in to the archives, took out Creative Creatures, dusted it off, and had a look to see whether its time had come? When Hanne, my business partner, and I launched it into the market place back in 2008, it felt new and different – a tool that helped individuals understand not if but how they were creative. It was based on research carried out at Sheffield University, it was uniquely branded, and it certainly stood out within the crowd of corporate frameworks.

Four or five years after launch, Hanne and I had decided to put Creative Creatures on the back burner for a while. As a new mother, she wanted to dedicate herself full-time to her daughter. As responsible parents, Mel and I had to dedicate much of our time to ours. However, we were all now slowly emerging from our respective hibernations.

In 2016, large companies were starting to spend more resource in the area of innovation and were looking for novel ways of achieving top line growth. The 2008 global financial crisis had now receded into the background, and a more optimistic outlook was emerging in many corporate boardrooms. Was the climate now right for Creative Creatures to tiptoe back out into the business arena?

And on a personal level, I had to decide whether to play things safe or give it a go. In the end, it all boiled down to what I wanted etched on my professional tombstone. I was faced with three options:

Option 1: Mark was a very good trainer who tried to be brave once, failed, and then played it safe for the rest of his career. He retired comfortably at the age of 70.

Option 2: Mark was a very good trainer who tried to be brave once, tried a second time, failed again, went bankrupt and spent the rest of his days living with a slightly disgruntled Mel in a caravan up in the wilds of Scotland.

Option 3; Mark was a very good trainer who tried to be brave once, tried a second time, and is now living in the South of France, aged 60.

I talked things through with Mel and we decided to aim for option 3. My Winner gene, with its receding hairline and paunch belly, was delighted by the decision and even my Worry gene knew it was the right option. What the hell, you only live once.

So, I took the plunge with Creative Creatures once again. I revisited all our old business contacts, reignited cold leads, chased up warm ones, started blogging, networking, opening new doors. All the usual stuff. At the same time, I set up a loose arrangement with two other colleagues and we worked together with an excellent agency called eatbigfish, getting something new and exciting off the ground. I also collaborated alongside other like-minded independents on projects for big-name clients.

I needed to have a few hot irons in the fire.

All in all, it was fun and refreshing, but money was still scarce, compared to previous years. For the first time in a career spanning two decades, I found myself under real financial pressure. And the timing wasn't great. Although two out of our three children had recently flown the nest, they were still cash consumers. Of our cash, that is. So, Mel and I had to make the same decisions most families are forced to make from time to time. In a nutshell, we had to work out how we could earn more and where we could spend less.

We agreed to give our new commercial ventures every possible chance to work out for the best which meant a lot of my work time would be spent investing in these and developing them, rather than chasing easier freelance money. As a consequence, I was working hard but not earning much.

Historically, Mel had always played a valuable role managing the back office of my business as an independent consultant. Now she had the time and space to take on more responsibilities for Creative Creatures too. She set up the database, started to learn a bit about social media and email marketing, carried out the analysis from the psychometric survey results as well as managing the accounts, both household and business. She took a lot of the pressure off me so that I could get on with the more generative side of things. We were dividing and conquering effectively. And although the business could not afford to pay her anything meaningful, we felt we were building something of value, albeit very slowly.

However, we were forced to dip in to our limited savings and we had the house valued just in case the downsizing option was required. Holidays were removed from the agenda. We didn't starve, but things were undeniably tight. The silver lining was this relative austerity pushed us to find pleasure in small and inexpensive ways.

An interesting concept Mel came up with was "wet August", the polar opposite to "dry January". A little luxury which gave us permission to indulge in an alcoholic drink or two every day for the entire month, rather than at weekends only. This was the normal "house rule" for the rest of the year. It was a concession that made us feel we were on holiday, without being on holiday, if you know what I mean. Fortunately for our livers, we were no better at sticking to the discipline of a wet August than many people are with their dry Januaries.

However, we spent all summer on the Costa Stewkley.

Somewhat refreshingly, 2016 and 2017 felt a bit like a sabbatical. I wasn't travelling excessively, I was busy trying to kick-start two business ventures, which meant pushing myself into new areas, meeting new people, trying out new ideas and

concepts. I also made more time available for my three children. I spent many hours with each of them either helping with exam revision, advising them on CVs and Personal Statements or guiding them through the job application process. It was a convenient time in all their lives for me not to be flying around the globe.

I just had to pretend that not earning enough money was not a problem. One tactic I found useful was never asking Mel how much we had in the bank account. Just like an ostrich, I was able to bury my head in the sand for a while. The bad news was it couldn't remain buried there forever. At some point, I would have to look up and address the realities of a dwindling bank balance.

During my sabbatical of sorts, I was also able to help Mel out on an emotional level. Five years on, Emily's illness had begun to take its toll on her. Knock back after knock back, false start after false start, tricky conversation after tricky conversation. It had all begun to affect her mood and disposition, and I felt she needed some help. Her wonderfully simple and rational way of seeing the world was making it more and more difficult for her to understand Emily's lack of progress. Playing Dolphin and St Bernard was becoming harder and harder, and more often than not, it was the Rhino / Terrier hybrid in her that held the upper hand.

261

I would still be called upon to play the mediator between wife and daughter, seeking the middle ground and trying to keep the peace between them. This was a critical time in Emily's recovery and I felt Mel's ability to be a more consistent and reliable Dolphin could have a significant bearing on the outcome. But I could sense she was struggling, and small hairline cracks were starting to appear. I felt it might benefit her to share her thoughts, her feelings, and her innermost frustrations with somebody who understood these things better than me. After much cajoling and persuading, she finally agreed to seek some professional help. She started seeing an insightful psychologist called Holly who helped coach her through the testing times she was still having with her daughter.

Each time she came home after one of her appointments, she would always tell us she had found the session very useful and that she felt she was making good progress. But she would also reassure us with a big grin on her face, that according to Holly, 'she wasn't the problem in the house, she was absolutely fine. It was us, we were the problem!' Mel's "happy gene" ensured that her sense of humour stayed intact throughout.

The irony was that I was now emotionally the strong one in the family, but it was a role I was absolutely delighted to assume. I still owed Mel big time.

With the notable exception of the income, 2016 and 2017 were proving to be two very rich years. In a strange way, I think I will be forever grateful my work as a freelancer dried up. It made me focus on what was really important, reassess my priorities in life, and add value to those around me whom I loved. I discovered purpose. Maybe it was this mindset shift that kept me mentally resilient when the pennies were short?

The banisters were firming up even through the lean times. I was learning that the more you embrace the tough times, the stronger you become. The downside was that it was now looking more and more likely that I would be getting that "caravan in Scotland with a disgruntled Mel" tombstone. And to be perfectly honest (and no disregard to the Scots), I preferred the warmth of the South of France.

Warrior Gene

However, it wasn't all plain sailing from a personal point of view. I was still challenged by my own character. There was one unexpected by-product of our precarious financial situation and my continued determination to end up under the right tombstone. A late entrant into the story but a significant one, which manifested itself mainly in the business arena. Spurred on by my new-found drive and ambition, I found myself caught up in more and more stressful situations which sometimes ended up in ugly confrontations. Conflict and confrontation were part and parcel of the corporate world, but in the past I had always stayed well clear of them wherever possible. They weren't really in my nature.

The late entrant to the scene was Warrior, the third of the "tricky" genes. Warrior was a feisty little creature. He had more Rhino and Terrier in him than he did either Dolphin or St Bernard. He didn't really understand the important difference between aggressive and assertive when it came to debate. He would "kick off" whenever he thought somebody was being unreasonable or just wasn't playing fair game. It wasn't so much the content of what he was saying that could be criticised, it was more the tone and the timing.

Warrior gene was quite possibly a consequence of my life stage. I was now sliding towards my 60s, and I wasn't going to take "no shit from no one no more". I wasn't prepared to back down when I had the strong sense an injustice had taken place. I was happy to call out an individual if I felt it was justified. I was also prepared to suffer the fall-out that would inevitably take place as a result.

But Warrior gene did need careful supervision because his outbursts didn't make for very pretty viewing. Everyone took it in turns to make sure he never lost the plot completely. Mel, the children, close friends, and colleagues all had a role in keeping our new addition to the family in check.

Very occasionally, he would unleash one of his explosive temper tantrums on the social scene, even with the closest of our friends. Mel would be mortified by what she was witnessing. The piercing glare across the table in a restaurant would be followed by a rollicking in the car on the way home with threats of imminent divorce, and then a stony silence the next morning. And for some strange reason, she was never placated when I tried to excuse myself with, 'I just couldn't help it. I'm just passionate about what I believe. In any case, it wasn't me, it was Warrior.'

And although he was in need of some mentoring, I did have a real soft spot for Warrior gene. He wore his heart on his sleeve. His character fundamentally came from a good place.

(A short postscript: Unless I can persuade him to do some DNA testing, which is highly unlikely, I will never be able to prove the strong hunch I have. That he is the love child of Winner and Worry gene. If the former was driven by ambition and the latter weighed down by anxiety, then Warrior was fuelled by an equally powerful emotion that was a mix of the two. Anger.)

CHAPTER 19

THE HOTTEST OF HOT SUMMERS

2018 was the hottest summer on record in England, with average temperatures narrowly beating those seen in 1976.[56] It will be remembered for a six-week spell from the end of June to the second week of August when it consistently reached 30 degrees Centigrade and the sky was a sparkling blue every single day.

It seemed each work email I wrote on a Monday morning started off with something like, 'I hope you really enjoyed the fantastic weather we had again', and every email I wrote on a Friday always signed off with, 'Enjoy the sunny weekend, I look forward to catching up next week'. It was a glorious period, with countless evenings spent outside in the garden soaking up the last rays of sunshine and every Saturday and Sunday getting up bright and early simply because you wanted to be outside rather than inside. There had to be something very wrong with you if you didn't have a permanent smile spread right across your face in the summer of 2018.

The first nine months of the year had also been very good to us as a family, with one sad exception, which I will come to later.

Will, Jack, Emily, and Purdey

Will was making his way through his accountancy training at KPMG in London, getting his head down and wading through the exams. Just before he left home the previous September to begin his first job in the City, I sat him down and gave him a little "dad pep talk" in the local pub. I told him it was important to forge a career in an area he liked, but it was equally important to play hard at the same time. I had done neither for much of my twenties. He gave me a somewhat bemused and blank look as if I was stating the obvious. He had a lovely girlfriend, a wide circle of friends, and knew exactly how to live a balanced life. He was far more skilled at this than I was at his age. He seemed very clear where he was going and how to get there. He thanked me for my advice and that marked a swift end to that part of the conversation. He seemed to have no further desire to know what else I had failed to do when I had been 23. So we had another beer and talked more sport.

Jack had finished his A Levels in the summer of 2017 when he informed us he didn't want to go to university. He was 18. He had a couple of firm business ideas he wanted to pursue and was much more motivated in becoming an entrepreneur than working for a large organisation. Many of our friends took their hats off to Jack and applauded what he was trying to do. We were all from the generation when career paths were predictable, and I think we were slightly envious we couldn't rewind the clock and do something different. However, having developed and launched a car reviewing website with his best mate during his gap year, Jack decided he needed to gain more experience in the wider business world. He recognised he still had an awful lot to learn, and so he started to look for a digital marketing apprenticeship.

As our youngest son oscillated, Mel and I kept faith. Our daughter's long illness had taught us the line through life is not always a straight one. Jack was discovering this for himself.

At the end of November, Jack secured an apprenticeship with an exclusive hotel group in London. He would be joining his two siblings in the capital.

Ana Goes to Prison

In 2018, Emily went from strength to strength. We visited her more and more in London and she would take us to her favourite restaurants. No, these weren't always Steakhouses or Pizzerias. Yes, they were often quirky little restaurants off the beaten track where vegetarian dishes were the main alternatives on offer. But it's only parents who have endured the pain of watching their children wither away in the grip of an eating disorder who will truly understand the relief of watching them sit down happily with a plate of food in front of them, and finish off every single morsel on the plate without a pained expression on their face.

In August, Emily got a promotion at work. She became a junior researcher on Loose Women, a daytime show on ITV. She had moved up from the bottom rung of the ladder and she had done so through sheer bloody-minded determination. I, Mel, Will, and Jack, as well as all the friends and family who had followed Emily on her painful crusade, were just so proud of her. She was slowly extricating herself from Ana's grip. Saying goodbye and good riddance.

In September 2018, the full-blown Anorexia Wars were slowly coming to an end. The illness had lasted six long years and during that time it had pretty much ruled our lives. We now finally believed anorexia nervosa might not dictate the rest of them. Although it was a silver lining I would not have wished for, the illness had also served to strengthen my own banisters. And Mel's. We were under no illusion other families had far greater burdens to deal with than the one that we were given. But we had been dealt a tricky hand, nonetheless. Mel and I didn't always get things right, but we took hard decisions when they needed to be taken and we never ducked the issue. We simply couldn't afford to. Too much was always at stake.

Both of us knew there were still likely to be skirmishes every now and then. We were also fully aware that war could break out again sometime in the future. We strongly suspected Ana would never be fully defeated. We had friends who had suffered from anorexia in their youth and they warned us to take nothing for granted. As a good friend described it, all we could hope was "that Ana will get incarcerated and gagged in a small section deep in Emily's brain, a high security area from which she can never escape".

Our daughter may or may not ever reach the very top of Mount Everest, but she had got herself to within a few feet. Well done, Emily. It was time for her to soak up the view, breathe in the mountain air, and start enjoying life. For now, the war was just about over. Just one final thing I need to get off my chest.

Fuck you, Ana. Fuck you.

Doggie Heaven

The only significant little blip the family suffered in the first six months of 2018 was when Purdey, our wonderful black Labrador, went to doggie heaven. She had played a good innings and had almost made it to her 15th birthday. If you're a dog lover, you'll know it's only when they're gone that you fully realise how much a part of your life they've been. And she was certainly our comfort blanket, in particular during the anorexia years when she provided Mel with constant companionship in the home. She was also my trusted walking partner when I needed to escape the house for an hour of "me-time" in order to recharge my own batteries.

When we sensed Purdey's time was close, but her hunger remained undiminished, we would always cave in and give her more than the occasional titbit or two in between her meals. She deserved it. The good news is that we can now imagine her "upstairs", lying peacefully at my mother's feet. Alice would be indulging in one of her favourite pastimes, enjoying a couple of "ciggies", while slipping a contented-looking Purdey a biscuit or two.

Creative Creatures Comes Out of Hibernation

In 2018, on the work front, we were blessed with an entire convoy of buses all turning up at the same time. Business boomed as all the seeds we had planted during the fallow years of 2016 and 2017 started to bear fruit. Hanne, my business partner, and Creative Creatures were both full of the joys of spring, ready to do great things. We were joined by Anita Dalsgaard, a 32-year-old expert in social media and digital marketing, and suddenly, our small boutique agency was being engaged by some big companies: Unilever, Diageo, Colgate Palmolive, GlaxoSmithKline, and the brewing giant ABInBev. We were not just working with top class companies and clients, but we were also getting involved in exciting projects that were stretching our creative brains to the limits. And most important of all, our mission was founded on a strong and single-minded purpose. We wanted to help every individual maximise their creative potential both in the professional and personal arenas.

It wasn't just about the money.

Having said that, Mel and I were relieved the bank balance was looking healthy again. Our accountant also breathed a sigh of relief. Downsizing to release some cash was no longer being discussed. Mel was able to go back to shopping at Waitrose with confidence, and we even managed to afford the luxury of two short breaks abroad during the summer of 2018.

I realised the business world could be both fickle and unpredictable and I was under no illusions our fortunes might change. Put it this way, I hadn't started looking at property prices in the South of France just yet. But this year, the corporate gods had been kind to us and both Mel's wine and Mark's beer were flowing once again. We were back to living the dream but working extremely hard at the same time.

Breakdown and Repair

The financial security we were enjoying took a huge burden off my mind. I now felt liberated to be at my best, and in 2018 the creative part of my brain was on fire. It was being bombarded with ideas 24 / 7. Einstein's combinatory play was back in town. It even got to the point where I would keep a Post-it pad and pen in the upstairs bathroom. Enjoying a shower first thing in the morning or a hot bath last thing at night were often when I seemed to be at my most inspired.

A typical day would go something like this: Wake up at half past six, go for a fast walk for an hour, work hard until three o'clock, have a compulsory 45-minute nap (my guilty pleasure), work hard until six o'clock. A bit of introvert time watching YouTube videos would be followed by dinner with Mel (TV still off), before watching one of the excellent police dramas on playback at ten o'clock. A hot bath and some bedtime reading would round off a full but balanced day. Pure bliss.

Worry gene had learnt to worry less (possibly an age thing) and Winner gene had learnt to operate safely within certain boundaries. But, interestingly, those boundaries had now been stretched, and the playing field had been expanded to a size I had never enjoyed before. I was no longer avoiding difficult conversations with friends, business partners, and clients, and this increased the scope of what was possible. And even though Warrior gene might misbehave from time to time, I felt better having the conversation than avoiding it.

I don't think it was the financial security alone that gave me this confidence. I think there were two other things at play. Firstly, the banisters. The last six years had served to strengthen them significantly. We had taken on Ana and we had beaten her in the bloodiest of wars. The struggle had given both Mel and me strong doses of resolve and resilience. We had been on an incredible journey that required us to take big decisions in the worthiest of causes: the health of our daughter. Taking on tricky challenges in the business arena where it was only money at stake, was, by comparison, a walk in the park.

Somewhat ironically, Emily's breakdown and subsequent repair had contributed significantly to my own repair. If you can find meaning in suffering, both your own and the suffering of others, if you can give yourself completely to somebody else in greater need than you, then you will emerge a stronger person. This remains one of the most significant things I have learnt on my journey.

But I also continued to oil the banisters with all the usual day-to-day lubricants. I exercised plenty, rested sufficiently, and socialised lots. My three children continued to show me the way ahead in this respect. I was always on hand to help others struggling with mental problems of their own. I had learnt that an outward-looking perspective would keep me grounded. Too much introspection is never good for your health.

I do have a little confession to make though. When the going got tough in 2017, and quite a few big events all started kicking off at the same time, I asked the doctor whether I could go back on anti-depressants as a pre-emptive strike. He knew my history, he agreed with my self-diagnosis, and he prescribed 100mg of sertraline a day. I am still taking them today. I have no idea of the contribution they have played in keeping the banisters strong but to be honest, I don't really care. I know pills don't work for everyone, and I will wean myself off them at some point soon, but right now I don't want to risk upsetting the apple cart.

The second factor which gave me the confidence to just "go for it" surrounded my choice of tombstone. I was almost 56 and didn't want to exit life with a whimper. As long as my ambition didn't affect the health or happiness of either my family or me, I would prefer to fail gloriously rather than not try at all. Maybe I could see the Grim Reaper in the far distance and I really hoped he would grant me another 30 years or so. But, using the sporting metaphor, I wanted to make sure I didn't leave anything out on the pitch when the full-time whistle went.

Superwoman

If Emily won "Woman of the Year" in the Simmonds household in 2018 then Mel ran her a pretty close second. As far as guiding her daughter back towards the shore, she became a role model Dolphin. Once or twice a day, Emily would call her mum and talk about things still troubling her either in the workplace or on a personal level. These were either small anxieties linked to the illness or matters any daughter would want to discuss with her mother when embarking on a new adventure. Mel would remain incredibly patient, ensuring all her Terrier or Rhino tendencies remained locked up. My supporting role was to help Emily with fiddly office emails, CV updating, ongoing career advice, as well as holding her hand whenever she had the occasional wobble. As husband and wife, we were a strong team, dividing and conquering wisely.

As Creative Creatures began to take off in 2018, the amount of work began to increase significantly, and Mel started to play an increasingly important role. She got to grips with a whole bunch of important tasks which went far beyond the administrative humdrum of the back office. She carried out research for articles and blogposts, assumed direct contact with key clients, and helped finetune and edit key proposals before they went out to clients. Her confidence rose quickly the more responsibilities she took on.

Imagine suddenly being gifted three additional days a week, allowing you to get on with work that can really shift the direction of your business.

That's what our little agency got from Mel.

When Mel said, 'I will' back in 1992, I had certainly "lucked out". I had known this throughout our 26-year marriage, but never was it more obvious than now. There was this silly but amusing game called "Saints and Sinners" we sometimes played with our friends on evenings out. Every person would be asked to judge each of the other couples around the table. Who was the Saint, somebody perfect and beyond reproach, and who was the Sinner, somebody "batting above their average", who perhaps didn't contribute as much to the marriage as their partner?

Slightly intoxicated by the effect of drink, these made for quite interesting debates which tested people's loyalties. It was rarely black and white and there were often split votes among the group as to which partner was which. However, whenever it came to Mel and me, the discussion was always short and the group decision unanimous.

Fortunately, the alcohol managed to dull my disappointment.

Hand-holding. I just needed to close the loop on this. Unfortunately, we never quite cracked it. I have come to the conclusion that our hands are physically incompatible. They don't interlock properly. However, we have devised a four-step process that works for us. 1. Grab each other's hand; 2. Squeeze; 3. Hold, hold, hold; 4. And release. This gives us about 20 seconds of flesh contact time which is usually sufficient to signal how much we care for one another.

Sue and Holly

'Investing in yourself is the best investment you will ever make. It will not only improve your life, it will improve the lives of those around you.' Words from Robin Sharma, a Canadian writer.[57]

Aged 55 and 54 respectively, Mel and I decided to invest in ourselves. Every now and then, Mel would see Holly and I got back in touch with Sue who had guided me so skilfully towards Happyville 18 months after my Big Blip in 2001. There were two reasons for our investment decision, one reactive and the other proactive. Firstly, as business began to boom and my stress levels started rising, Warrior's temper tantrums were becoming slightly unpredictable. We both needed help trying to rein him in before he got himself into deep trouble.

Secondly, with the children out of the house and off our hands, we would soon have more disposable time. More time for each other, more time to tick off all the other things on our respective bucket lists. What was the harm in having the occasional conversation with two professionals who could help us make the right choices and bring out the best in us?

So once again, Mel and I turned to our respective "dive buddies", Holly and Sue, to help us grow just a little bit more.

The Secret of Life

So, as I slowly meander my way to the end of my tale, 2018 is also winding its way to a close. It has been a fulfilling year in many aspects of our life. We have felt very blessed. However, I have been around long enough to know the good times don't last forever. I distinctly remember that moment, 12 months after the golden summer of 2012 came to its glorious finale, thinking what a difference a year can make when Emily was being tortured by Ana, and our lives were being turned upside down.

Earlier in the book, I claimed, tongue in cheek, to have discovered the secret of life. 'As long as you are blessed with good health and a bit of luck, the route to happiness is firstly picking the right partner, secondly, choosing the right career, and then sticking with both.' As I reflect back on the last 18 years, I now believe that claim to be overly simplistic. Yes, choice of partners and profession are both important, but bad stuff can still happen all around you:

Illness, death in the family, the thought of death, heartache, a messy divorce, money worries, friendship issues, your favourite team getting relegated, the uncertainty of Brexit, the certainty of nothing, middle-aged acne, molehills decimating the garden ... It's how you cope with the bad stuff, both big and little, the nature of your relationship with it, and the attitude you adopt when dealing with it. That's what counts. That's what's required if you are to find the real secret to a happy life.

It's really all in the mind.

I know unforeseen challenges will be thrown our way in years to come. That is inevitable. But I am not quite so worried anymore. I believe I'm now better equipped with the mental resilience needed to withstand most things. I have found that the banisters put in place all those years back were made of hard teak.

But right now, right this minute, at the end of December 2018, my world is okay and I want to enjoy it. A lovely quote from Thornton Wilder, the American playwright and novelist, encapsulates a very healthy take on life:

'My advice to you is not to enquire why or whither, but just enjoy your ice cream while it's on your plate – that's my philosophy.'[58]

We Are the Champions, My Friend

In my job as a management trainer, one thing I have been unable to completely crack is how to end a training course. How do you ensure every single person leaves the room with a smile on their face? You've been with the group for a few days, and hopefully it has gone very well. Everyone has learnt lots and had some fun along the way. You've made strong connections with the participants on a human level. It's four o'clock on the final day. They've completed their evaluation forms and you've just made your closing remarks, imparting your final pearls of wisdom. You thank them for their hard work and attention and wish them the best of luck ... and then what do you do? What now?

I have never been very sure about this bit. Usually, there is a moment or two of awkward silence before somebody from the group senses the unease, steps in, and starts clapping. Everyone else joins in, including myself and I applaud the group in a "I couldn't have done it without you" kind of way.

A colleague of mine has a very definitive way of ending a course. He plays a rousing song from his iPhone which is connected to a set of booming speakers. It's usually something upbeat and uplifting like 'We are the Champions' by Queen. It works for him, but it's not quite my style.

So, how do I now end this book in an uplifting kind of way? Which single-minded thought do I want implanted in the reader's mind as they close the book for the final time. There were two strong candidates. In second place, came Lewis Carroll's highly relevant line from *Alice in Wonderland*:

'You're entirely bonkers. But I'll tell you a secret. All the best people are.'[59]

But I figured that wasn't wholly appropriate because it might not resonate with everybody else in the same way it does with me.

However, there was an undisputed and outright winner.

If there was just one person from the world of entertainment I would like to have met during my lifetime to say thank you to, it would have been Robin Williams, the great American comedian and actor. He starred in so many inspiring films like *Good Morning Vietnam*, *Dead Poet's Society*, *Mrs. Doubtfire*, and *Good Will Hunting*. And he had that wonderful ability to make you laugh and cry, sometimes at the same time. He was a genius.

Tragically in 2014, at the age of 63 in his California home, he died by suicide. During his life, he had suffered from alcohol and drug addiction as well as depression and dementia. He was a troubled soul at the end. But didn't he achieve a lot during his career despite his many problems and challenges! What an incredible life's work. What a legacy to anybody with a sense of humour or a sense of soul.

So, the one short message of his I want to leave behind is aimed at all those people out there who currently suffer from mental ill health, of any form, and those who have suffered in the past.

If you view this as a problem, a burden on society, or any kind of limiting factor, please don't. It's not.

It really isn't.

You must see it as your unique gift to the world.

You're only given a little spark of madness.
You mustn't lose it.'

Robin Williams[60]

ACKNOWLEDGEMENTS

During my Big Blip, these were the close friends who were always there for Mel and me in the darkest of days: Mark and Chris, Jane and Philip, Sally and Simon; Chris and Lizzy; Mike and Lou; Oliver; Mick.

Sue, you gave me the banisters I needed in the years that followed.

And when the Anorexia Wars were raging, Emily's closest friends never left her side: Harri; Charissa, Eilis, Frankie, Kate, Kelly, Louise, Maddie, Myffi, Lola and Sophie, Hannah Jess, Izzy, Emily E, Emily S.

Benny and Susie G, you both stepped in when my daughter was on the ropes, in need of urgent help.

Over the last eighteen years, Pat and Doug, you kept us all grounded whenever the road became bumpy (Seagulls!).

To doctors Dunford, Gibby, Silverman, their wonderful colleagues at Ashcroft Surgery, and all the other medical professionals who helped us out, both in the NHS and in the private sector: an enormous Thank You.

And as for the book ...

Kasim, my editor. You saw the potential in the book and steered me down the right paths. Cath from Fusion Graphic Design, you did a terrific job on its design. Richard M, thank you so much for putting me in touch with Trigger. I owe you!

Lucy, your illustrations brought endless smiles to my face. It was such fun working with you!

David and Deborah, Jeff and Fi, David and Jill, Birksy, Rodders: you were all fearsome critics (!) and provided me with the open and honest sounding board advice I required.

Susan, Sam, Tony, Hilary, Jo, Andy S, Andy B and Mhairi: you ensured that the Brand Learning story was an accurate, fair and balanced one.

I would also like to thank those people who very kindly agreed to endorse the book, as well as everyone who took the time to read it: Mia, Jamie, Olly R, Richard H, Justin B, Matthew D, Chris A, Claire, Eion, Emily F, Sarah and Ian P, Sue and David S, Katie and Matilda from the Wellcome Shop. Your feedback was appreciated and valued.

A special debt of gratitude to Alan, Antony, Mark and Simon. Your experience, expertise and wisdom gave me reassurance when I most needed it.

The "Truswell sub-editorial team" - Graham, Mel, Susie, Alastair (and Lorna in spirit): without your enormous contribution and patience, the book would still be a work in progress.

... and finally, a very special thank you to Alice and Peter, my long-departed parents: you gifted me the tricky genes. They were a blessing and most definitely NOT a burden.

REFERENCES

1. **Muhlheim, L.** (2017). *Perfectionism in Eating Disorders.* Retrieved from https://www.verywellmind.com/perfectionism-in-anorexia-nervosa-1138391. [accessed 07/12/19]
2. **Bardone-Cone, A.** (2009). *Perfectionism across stages of recovery from eating disorders.* Retrieved from https://onlinelibrary.wiley.com/doi/abs/10.1002/eat.20674. [accessed 07/12/19]
3. **Sample, I.** (2018). *'Gene map for depression' sparks hopes of new generation of treatments.* Retrieved from www.theguardian.com/science/2018/apr/26/gene-map-for-depression-sparks-hopes-of-new-generation-of-treatments. [accessed 07/12/19]
4. **Goodreads.** (2019). *Work quotes.* Retrieved from www.goodreads.com/quotes/tag/work. [accessed 07/12/19]
5. **YourTango.** (2016). *20 Love, Life and Heartbreak Quotes from Leo Christopher.* Retrieved from www.yourtango.com/2016285230/20-love-life-and-heartbreak-quotes-leo-christopher.[accessed 07/12/19]
6. **Rampton, J.** (2015). *23 of the Most Amazingly Successful Introverts in History.* Retrieved from www.inc.com/john-rampton/230-amazingly-successful-introverts-throughout-history.html. [accessed 07/12/19]
7. **Balachandar, S.** (2016). *Who is an extrovert?* Retrieved from www.quora.com/Who-is-an-extrovert#. [accessed 07/12/19]
8. **Prater, M.** (2018). *25 Steve Jobs Quotes That Will Dramatically Shift Your Mindset.* Retrieved from https://blog.hubspot.com/sales/steve-jobs-quotes. [accessed 07/12/19]
9. **Schultz, E.** (2015). *Johnnie Walker Makes Big Changes to 'Keep Walking'.* Retrieved from https://adage.com/article/cmo-strategy/johnnie-walker-makes-big-walking/300411/. [accessed 07/12/19]
10. **Wei W.** (2012). *Move Over, Paul Ryan – This Is How Barack Obama Stays In Amazing Shape.* Retrieved from www.businessinsider.com/barack-obamas-workout-routine-2012-8?r=UK&IR=T. [accessed 07/12/19]
11. **Magazine.** (2003). *Oprah's Boot Camp.* Retrieved from www.oprah.com/omagazine/oprah-gets-fit-her-workout-routine.[accessed 07/12/19]
12. **Kim S.** (2016). *What really happens to your body on a flight.* Retrieved from www.telegraph.co.uk/travel/news/travel-advice-what-happens-to-your-body-o n-a-flight-travel-health/ [accessed 07/12/19]

13. **Gupta T.** (2015). *Magna Carta: Runnymede, the meadow where history was made*. Retrieved from www.bbc.co.uk/news/uk-england-surrey-32828251. [accessed 07/12/19]

14. **Famous Poets and Poems.** (2010). *Victor Hugo Quotes*. Retrieved from http://famouspoetsandpoems.com/poets/victor_hugo/quotes. [accessed 07/12/19]

15. **Orendorff, A.** (2018). *The Dark Side of Entrepreneurship: 2018 Data & Resources for Help*. Retrieved from www.shopify.com/enterprise/the-dark-side-of-entrepreneurship-that-nobody-wants-to-talk-about. [accessed 07/12/19]

16. **Gray R.** (2017). *How flying seriously messes with your mind*. Retrieved from www.bbc.com/future/story/20170919-how-flying-seriously-messes-with-your-mind. [accessed 07/12/19]

17. **Goodreads.** (2019). *Rita Mae Brown quotes*. Retrieved from www.goodreads.com/author/quotes/23511.Rita_Mae_Brown. [accessed 07/12/19]

18. **Brainy Quote.** (2019). *Desmond Tutu Quotes*. Retrieved from www.brainyquote.com/quotes/desmond_tutu_454129. [accessed 07/12/19]

19. **Goodreads.** (2019). *Ned Vizzini quotes*. Retrieved from www.goodreads.com/author/quotes/11672.Ned_Vizzini. [accessed 07/12/19]

20. **Goodreads.** (2019). *J.K. Rowling, quotes, quotable quote*. Retrieved from www.goodreads.com/quotes/388617-depression-is-the-most-unpleasant-thing-i-have-ever-experienced. [accessed 07/12/19]

21. **Richard, R.** (2017). *Effects of Stress on the Hippocampus and Memory*. Retrieved from https://sanescohealth.com/effects-of-stress-on-the-hippocampus-and-memory/. [accessed 07/12/19]

22. **Amsten, A.** (2010). *Stress signalling pathways that impair prefrontal cortex structure and function*. Retrieved from www.ncbi.nlm.nih.gov/pmc/articles/PMC2907136/. [accessed 07/12/19]

23. **Baglioni, C.** (2014). *Insomnia disorder is associated with increased amygdala reactivity to insomnia-related stimuli*. Retrieved from www.ncbi.nlm.nih.gov/pubmed/25325493. [accessed 07/12/19]

24. **Atlas Obscura.** (2019). *Aokigahara Suicide Forest*. Retrieved from www.atlasobscura.com/places/aokigahara-suicide-forest. [accessed 07/12/19]

25. **Goodreads.** (2019). *Ranata Suzuki, quotes, quotable quote*. Retrieved from www.goodreads.com/quotes/8399617-there-comes-a-point-where-you-no-longer-care-if. [accessed 07/12/19]

26. **Skoutelas, C.** (2017). *Think Suicide Is Selfish? Here's Why You've Got It All Wrong*. Retrieved from www.huffpost.com/entry/think-suicide-is-selfish-heres-why-youve-got-it_b_59223a3ce4b07617ae4cbd77. [accessed 07/12/19]

27. **Goodreads.** (2019). *Winston S. Churchill quotes*. Retrieved from www.goodreads.com/author/quotes/14033.Winston_S_Churchill?page=2. [accessed 07/12/19]

28. **Channel 4.** (2010). *Chile miners rescue in quotes*. Retrieved from www.channel4.com/news/chile-miners-rescue-in-quotes. [accessed 07/12/19]

29. **Goodreads.** (2019). *Lemony Snicket, quotes, quotable quote*. Retrieved from www.goodreads.com/quotes/4735-fate-is-like-a-strange-unpopular-restaurant-filled-with-odd. [accessed 07/12/19]

30. **Wellbeing.** (2017). *Mental Health at Work Report 2017*. Retrieved from https://wellbeing.bitc.org.uk/system/files/research/bitcmental_health_at_work_report-2017.pdf. [accessed 07/12/19]

31. **Merriam-Webster.** (2019). *Decompression sickness*. Retrieved from www.merriam-webster.com/dictionary/decompression%20sickness. [accessed 07/12/19]

32. **Wilson, H.** (2011). *Antonio Horta-Osario: the bank chief who just could not switch off*. Retrieved from www.telegraph.co.uk/finance/newsbysector/banksandfinance/8959785/Antonio-Horta-Osorio-the-bank-chief-who-just-could-not-switch-off.html. [accessed 07/12/19]

33. **Hutchinson, S.** (2013). *6 Common Myths About Sharks, Debunked*. Retrieved from http://mentalfloss.com/article/52130/6-common-myths-about-sharks-debunked. [accessed 07/12/19]

34. **Goodreads.** (2019). *Sade Andria Zabala quotes*. Retrieved from www.goodreads.com/author/quotes/6906487.Sade_Andria_Zabala. [accessed 07/12/19]

35. **Oxford Dictionaries.** (2019). *Strategy*. Retrieved from https://en.oxforddictionaries.com/definition/strategy. [accessed 07/12/19]

36. **Jeffries, S.** (2008). *'I've always liked an unsettled life'*. Retrieved from www.theguardian.com/lifeandstyle/2008/mar/07/women.theobserver. [accessed 07/12/19]

37. **Farnam Street.** (2019). *Einstein on the Essential Feature of Productive Thought*. Retrieved from https://fs.blog/2014/04/einstein-productive-thought-combinatory-creativity/. [accessed 07/12/19]

38. **Muscolino, J.** (2014). *Raise a Towel to Douglas Adam with These 9 Stellar Quotes*. Retrieved from www.signature-reads.com/2014/03/raise-a-towel-to-douglas-adams-with-these-9-stellar-quotes/. [accessed 07/12/19]

39. **Encyclopaedia Brittanica.** (2018). *Sir William Withey Gull, 1st Baronet*. Retrieved from www.britannica.com/biography/Sir-William-Withey-Gull-1st-Baronet. [accessed 07/12/19]

40. **Hodgman, C.** (1978). *The Golden Cage: The Enigma of Anorexia Nervosa*. Retrieved from yjamanetwork.com/journals/jamapediatrics/article-abstract/508049. [accessed 07/12/19]

41. **Lyons, L.** (2017). *Genetic Factors Behind Eating Disorders*. Retrieved from www.eatingdisorderhope.com/blog/genetic-factors-eating-disorders. [accessed 07/12/19]

42. **Priory Group.** (2019). *Eating Disorder Statistics*. Retrieved from www.priorygroup.com/eating-disorders/eating-disorder-statistics. [accessed 07/12/19]

43. **Hamilton, G.** (2019). *Anorexia Nervosa – Highest Mortality Rate of any Mental Disorder: Why?* Retrieved from www.eatingdisorderhope.com/information/anorexia/anorexia-nervosa-highest-mortality-rate-of-any-mental-disorder-why. [accessed 07/12/19]

44. **Quote Fancy.** (2019). *Elizabeth Gilbert.* Retrieved from https://quotefancy.com/quote/801278/Elizabeth-Gilbert-Embrace-the-glorious-mess-that-you-are. [accessed 07/12/19]

45. **Urban Dictionary.** (2019). *Lemming.* Retrieved from www.urbandictionary.com/define.php?term=lemming. [accessed 07/12/19]

46. **Motluk, A.** (2007). *Starving is like ecstasy use for anorexia sufferers.* Retrieved from www.newscientist.com/article/dn12718-starving-is-like-ecstasy-use-for-anorexia-sufferers/. [accessed 07/12/19]

47. **Cardinal Clinic.** (2019). Retrieved from https://cardinalclinic.co.uk/ [accessed 07/12/19]

48. **National Institutes of Health.** (2019). *What People With Anorexia Nervosa Need to Know About Osteoporosis.* Retrieved from www.bones.nih.gov/health-info/bone/osteoporosis/conditions-behaviors/anorexia-nervosa. [accessed 07/12/19]

49. **Collins Dictionary.** (2019). *Definition of 'no-man's land'.* Retrieved from www.collinsdictionary.com/dictionary/english/no-mans-land. [accessed 07/12/19]

50. **AZ Quotes.** (2019). *Chris Guillebeau Quotes.* Retrieved from www.azquotes.com/author/19227-Chris_Guillebeau. [accessed 07/12/19]

51. **Tumblr. (2019).** Resilience quotes. Retrieved from www.tumblr.com/search/resilience%20quotes. [accessed 07/12/19]

52. **Oxford Health.** (2019). *Cotswold House Oxford Inpatient Unit.* Retrieved from www.oxfordhealth.nhs.uk/cotswoldhouse/service/oxford-inpatient/. [accessed 07/12/19]

53. **Time to Change.** (2019). *Alastair Campbell talks about depression.* Retrieved from www.time-to-change.org.uk/news-media/celebrity-supporters/alastair-campbell. [accessed 07/12/19]

54. **Fishel, B.** (2017). Retrieved from www.projectmonkeymind.com/2017/07/viktor-frankl-quotes-meaning-life-love-suffering/ [accessed 07/12/19]

55. **Michael Neill.** (2019). The Principles Behind the Human Experience. Retrieved from www.michaelneill.org/introduction/the-principles-behind-the-human-experience/. [accessed 07/12/19]

56. **Griffin, A.** (2018). Summer 2018 was hottest ever, Met Office announces. Retrieved from www.independent.co.uk/news/science/summer-2018-hottest-ever-england-uk-met-office-announcement-latest-a8520746.html. [accessed 07/12/19]

57. **Goodreads.** (2019). Robin S. Sharma quotes. Retrieved from www.goodreads.com/quotes/493669-investing-in-yourself-is-the-best-investment-you-will-ever. [accessed 07/12/19]

58. **Khawaja, S.** (2016). Life According to Thornton Wilder (a collection of quotes). Retrieved from www.arts.gov/art-works/2016/life-according-thornton-wilder-collection-quotes. [accessed 07/12/19]

59. **Goodreads.** (2019). Alice in Wonderland quotes. Retrieved from www.goodreads.com/work/quotes/2933712-alice-in-wonderland. [accessed 07/12/19]

60. **Brainy Quote**. (2019). Robin Williams quotes. Retrieved from www.brainyquote.com/quotes/robin_williams_383381. [accessed 07/12/19]

If you found this book interesting ... why not read these next?

Teacup In A Storm

Finding My Psychiatrist

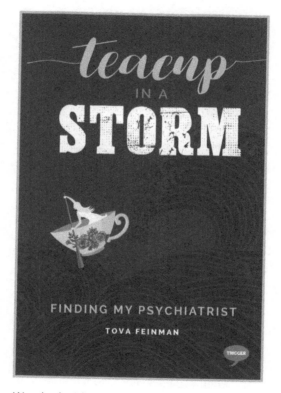

Wracked with trauma from childhood abuse, Tova sought therapy to soothe her mind. However, it is not as easy as simply finding a person to talk to ...

This Too Will Pass

Anxiety in a Professional World

What happens when you have a breakdown? Can you ever pick up the pieces? Or do you have to create a whole new life for yourself? Richard's book answers those questions.

the *Shaw* mind
FOUNDATION

Creating hope for children,
adults and families

Sign up to our charity, The Shaw Mind Foundation
www.shawmindfoundation.org
and keep in touch with us; we would love to hear
from you.

*We aim to bring to an end the suffering and despair caused
by mental health issues. Our goal is to make help and support
available for every single person in society, from all walks of
life. We will never stop offering hope. These are our promises.*

TRIGGER™

The mental health & wellbeing publisher

www.triggerpublishing.com

Trigger is a publishing house devoted to opening conversations about mental health. We tell the stories of people who have suffered from mental illnesses and recovered, so that others may learn from them.

Adam Shaw is a worldwide mental health advocate and philanthropist. Now in recovery from mental health issues, he is committed to helping others suffering from debilitating mental health issues through the global charity he co-founded, The Shaw Mind Foundation. www.shawmindfoundation.org

Lauren Callaghan (CPsychol, PGDipClinPsych, PgCert, MA (hons), LLB (hons), BA), born and educated in New Zealand, is an innovative industry-leading psychologist based in London, United Kingdom. Lauren has worked with children and young people, and their families, in a number of clinical settings providing evidence based treatments for a range of illnesses, including anxiety and obsessional problems. She was a psychologist at the specialist national treatment centres for severe obsessional problems in the UK and is renowned as an expert in the field of mental health, recognised for diagnosing and successfully treating OCD and anxiety related illnesses in particular. In addition to appearing as a treating clinician in the critically acclaimed and BAFTA award-winning documentary *Bedlam*, Lauren is a frequent guest speaker on mental health conditions in the media and at academic conferences. Lauren also acts as a guest lecturer and honorary researcher at the Institute of Psychiatry Kings College, UCL.